Angels

Visions

Miracles

Dreams

The Journey with Jesus Series

Book One

By Sheri Locke Smith

D1522344

Dedicated

to

The Holy Spirit

Who guided me through

the completion of this book.

Special thanks to my husband

Gary Smith

A great believer who lived it all with me

and

my daughter

Sally Henry

Who kept me grounded and encouraged.

Table of Contents

Preface- The Vision

Chapters

Here we go...

I don't know when my true love for God started. I know I was young. Looking back there are so many times that He was there for me, intersecting in the lows and highs of my life. I always believed in Him but was not necessarily raised to treat Him as my friend who was there to instruct, comfort, care and look out for me in general, on a day to day basis.

I always prayed. I always asked forgiveness…yet I never really thought of doing something back for Him. Always inspired by His Greatness and yet oblivious to how He would love me so continuously , so always there for me in every little way, without the true acknowledgement that today I know He deserves and loves.

Over the years there are many things I have taken for granted time and time again and called them the result of coincidence or my own effort. Time after time I did this until one day He saved my life in such an obvious way that I could no longer live for anyone but Him.

I had a vision.

Preface... The Vision

In my spirit I saw the pages of an old and antiquated book fanning open. When it stopped, a hand came down and pointed with index finger to these words.

Jeremiah 1

The Prophet Is Called

4 Then the word of the Lord came to me, saying:
5 "Before I formed you in the womb I knew you;
Before you were born I sanctified you;
I ordained you a prophet to the nations."
6 Then said I:
"Ah, Lord God!
Behold, I cannot speak, for I *am* a youth."
7 But the Lord said to me:
"Do not say, 'I *am* a youth,'
For you shall go to all to whom I send you,

And whatever I command you, you shall speak.
8 Do not be afraid of their faces,
For I *am* with you to deliver you," says the Lord.
9 Then the Lord put forth His hand and touched my
mouth, and the Lord said to me:
"Behold, I have put My words in your mouth.
10 See, I have this day set you over the nations and
over the kingdoms,
To root out and to pull down,
To destroy and to throw down,
To build and to plant."

What did I just see?

That was so unexpected and I immediately got up from
bed to look over the scripture that was just presented to
me in my spirit. It was very profound.

A Prophet? I had a lot to learn.

This book is about the journey.

My Journey.

My Journey with Jesus!

Chapter 1

The recipe…The start was small…YET BIG.

I knew what a prophet was, but did not know how I fit that description.

By fall of 2010 I had finished a Bible and leadership training school offering an opportunity to be ordained upon completion. I was asked if I would be willing to preach on Wednesday nights and I agreed. The following summer I was ordained and was offered a position as Sunday Evening Pastor at the same church.

Now ours is a unique church, in that time period I think there were just three or so people in the entire church that had a license to operate an automobile. These people mostly had rough lives.

I liked to take food to church and often I would serve bread like my mother used to make.

My mother was a wonderful bread maker and although I watched her throughout the process all the time growing up I had not learned the recipe.

My mother had passed away so how could I get the recipe?

No one ever wrote down the recipe. Her bread was a gift, so light and perfect. A real treat when I was growing up and she would take it warm out of the oven and serve it to our family, her friends, and coworkers. with butter melting on it. The smell was as delicious, as the taste. She was known for her culinary skills.

Well, I was praying one night and basically thanking and delighting in the Lord. Eventually I got to it and asked the Lord if He could help me remember that recipe. If He could it would seem like all those hours of watching my mother would not have been in vain.

The next morning I knew the recipe.

I just knew it!

Interestingly at that point in my life even after wanting this so badly and not knowing it, I did not chalk the answer up to God.

Well, anyway, my mother got a lot of mileage out of this recipe. I started serving it to the church members after the morning service on a regular basis.

The following stories have some of the highlights of my amazing Journey with Jesus through visions, dreams, angels and miracles I have experienced.

As for the bread? I figured out that was a gift from God also! Give it a try. You will like it.

2

Now that recipe truly IS a gift from God!

I'll place the recipe in the back of the book for a guaranteed happy ending!

Key take away #1   Delight in the Lord.

Psalm 37:4
Take delight in the Lord and He will give you the desires of your heart!

Could it be so simple? Just delighting in the Lord and prayer?

I hope this book brings you delight, strengthens your faith and stretches your boundaries.

Chapter 2   The Dream

Well, I had a dream...about bread.

On a Saturday night, I had a very vivid dream. I went to an auction to buy the crock bowls of a wonderful neighbor lady that had passed away. Her actual name in real life was Neva Bowls. She was a neighbor lady, who was very sweet and had often babysat my kids.

In the dream I had gone to her estate auction. I looked at the bowls that I wished to purchase to fill with bread.

There were three bowls total. Each bowl had some damage. One was cracked, one was chipped here and there and another had a lot of stains.

I decided they were pretty attainable because who would want them?

I felt I did, if for no other reason than sentiment alone.

Even after thinking this though, I remember distinctly going to the auctioneer and expressing interest.

He showed me they were listed in the catalog and much interest had been expressed by others.

He said this auction would be different from other auctions as these bowls would go to the **LOWEST** bidder. Well, I remember thinking that I had never heard of that.

The **LOWEST** bidder!???!

I remember thinking,

"What would I bid???

If I bid five, someone could bid four?

Me three?

They two?

Me one?

Would they let the others bid 50 cents?"

I specifically remember this bidding debate within myself without knowing what to do.

Meanwhile, while I was pondering all these price options and bidding decisions in the dream, I realized I had missed bidding for the bowls altogether.

The auctioneer had passed them by already.

I questioned him about it and he told me I was too late.

Too late?!

They were gone, and **no one had bid low** enough!

There was more to the dream but this is the important part and then I awoke.

Silly dream, I thought as I walked into the bathroom and took a bath. All the while I was bathing though, I kept thinking of the dream.

It just stayed in my head.

I was to preach that morning as one of the pastors of The Church of the Living Water and was getting dressed and ready for the service.

Standing before a mirror, putting curlers in my hair, I heard the **voice.**

As clear as if you were speaking with me in the same room, a voice said

"Go back to bed" and "Take a Pen."

I went back to bed.

I took a pen. The voice continued and spoke similarly as I wrote.

Yes, the bowls you wanted were, cracked, broken, and stained.

They were not always that way,

they had, had a very hard life, BUT,

they were all still able to hold bread,

"The Word of God."

They were important to Me, too!

They had sentimental value to Me, too!

I loved each one very, very much!

Each was uniquely special and very much able to hold the bread of life.

 Now it is too late because no one would get "low" (humble) enough to take interest in these vessels and now they are lost forever.

Key take away #2   Listen to and discern your dreams.

The bible says

John 6 [51] I am the living bread which came down from heaven. If anyone eats of this bread, he will live forever; and the bread that I shall give is My flesh, which I shall give for the life of the world."

Wow and Amen! A sermon was to come from my mouth in less than an hour and I just had the **Holy Spirit, God, Jesus** tell me that which seemed like one very random dream, was one of the biggest lessons of my life to date!

So humbled, yes, I went before the church and told them everything that had been told to me earlier that morning.

I would never, ever be the same after that day and hour. Neither would the church!

Well, from that day forward I was continuously reminded to ask myself am I low/humble enough?

Do I bypass someone just because they appear cracked, broken or stained?

How easily that we could be any one of these vessels.

Any one of us!

Do you pass them by? It's something to think about.

Decisions like this can be the difference between the eternal bread of life being placed in any one of the people we cross paths with daily or perhaps that person being lost forever.

That is a very big lesson and responsibility if you can grasp it.

Something to strive toward for sure!

Well, we got pretty excited about our dreams, all of us in the congregation and we all started taking pen and paper to bed, writing down everything!

Who wanted to miss lessons like these?

Acts 2:17

"In the last days, God says, I will pour out my Spirit on all people. Your sons and daughters will prophesy, your young men will see visions, your old men will dream dreams.

Numbers 12:6

He said, "Listen to my words: "When there is a prophet among you, I the Lord, reveal myself to them in visions, I speak to them in dreams.

Daniel 7:1

In the first year of Belshazzar king of Babylon, Daniel had a dream, and visions passed through his mind as he was lying in bed. He wrote down the substance of his dreams.

Chapter 3 **The Fallout**

The questions…and fallout

The fallout…well, it went over very well but apparently that story was a little much (out there) for a couple of people in the congregation. Some judgmental comments came back to me and it really hurt. I went home and cried. I actually got upset with the Lord and in an upset manner told him I do not know anyone in person with this gift!!

"Why me?" I said, remember this was very early in my walking in the gifts

The church in which I was raised did not necessarily focus on the gifts at all.

If I just knew one person it would help! I was new in my walk with the Lord and without knowing anyone else with this ability how will I be any more than the crazy lady at church?!

"Why me?" I said to Him again.

" Why do I not know anyone who has heard from you aloud?"

Just then I saw the number 212 ### #### come before me. I could not shake the number out of my head.

Generally speaking my memory is not so good, but there was no getting this ten digit number out of my mind.

A half hour later after taking a bath, and without having written it down it was still in my head, so I set to figure it out!

Was it scripture? I tried counting letters to align with numbers, to make it out as scripture but to no avail.

What if I type it into the internet?

Nothing!

Nothing!?!

Thinking, I tried dialing it into the phone

and I tapped into a phone call already in progress.

They could not hear me but I could hear them. It was like the old days when we had a party line and you could just pick up the receiver and listen in to a chat / conference call already in progress.

There were many voices and the persons participating in the call were holy people, citing verse and scripture and preceding much with" Thus Saith the Lord". Listening intently, I could not believe it.

Occasionally, I would speak up and say hello just in case the people on the other end of the call might hear me. I was learning so much. Able to hear them, yet they could not hear me, what was happening?

It turns out it was a group of prophets having a meeting through a conference call. Sharing their visions, dreams, and declaring the Word of the Lord. Each backed their declarations with scripture. I was absorbing this as fast as I could.

There came a point in time where they decided to take a break for supper or bathroom or both. Turns out this was happening at least from the teachers end, from the location of New York City.

What seemed to be the moderator or head prophetess teaching the class and leading the discussion (yes they were referring to each other as prophets) had each of those participating, sign off in a roll call style manner.

This was called out by the person they called Prophetess Kelly. She called out the last of them by name and they signed off and told each one what time to be back to resume their call. I had learned so much!

I was so thankful to the Lord for showing this to me! It was so amazing, comforting, and a huge learning experience. I realized through eavesdropping that my gifts were similar to their gifts and I was quite emboldened.

As the last of the prophets signed off of the call with Prophetess Kelly, I said hello one more time just because.

Low and behold this time the head Prophetess heard me. Embarrassed to have been caught listening in to a class/call that I had neither paid for nor been invited to, I started to apologize, and tell her I was sorry but she interrupted me by saying,

"Have you been listening?"

"Listening?" I said ,"Yes" and once again started to apologize, feeling like a real interloper when she asked if I had been listening in?

"Are you from Iowa?" she asked.

I said "Yes"

"Uh Oh", I thought and then she said...now remember she is in New York City.

"Are you from Iowa?"

I was in disbelief how did she know this?

Then came the zinger of all zingers

She said, "Is this Sheri?"

"What? Yes," I said, "but how did you know?"

"This is Gloria, Sheri! Your old college roommate!"

Silence!

Silence!

Silence!

Blown away, I immediately went to tears, not only had God shown me someone I knew with prophetic gifting's that He also called a prophet but

He showed me, by letting me find one of my best friends from college whom I had lost track of years before and searched for, for many, many years.

This was the most gentle and loving way that the Lord could have allowed me to process the title of Prophet He had given me without my initial understanding of all it entailed.

I knew her as Gloria Smith who had moved to Kansas City, but did not know she had moved to New York and married a man named Don Kelly. I knew him (Don) only by the nickname of Buddha, a silly nickname from college.

I was in such shock. No way could I have found someone with the last name of Kelly or Smith in New York City, had I even known. We exchanged emails with each other as a witness to the miracle and promised to keep in touch. This made for an exciting sermon. I had so much to tell the congregation. They must believe me.

15

God was so real!

God was still communicating and Now I was sure ALL things are possible with God! With renewed spirit I embraced my new title He had shown me and did not look back!

What a journey!

Key takeaway #3.   **Don't listen to the devil. God's got your back!**

Matthew 19:26
But Jesus looked at them and said to them, "With men this is impossible, but with God **all** things are possible."

Numbers 12:6 He said, "Listen to my words: When there is a prophet among you, I the Lord, reveal myself to them in visions, I speak to them in dreams."

Chapter 4   Rhema words

Soon thereafter I had an extraordinary experience that I will never forget. I was lying in bed, encouraged and loving every bit of this unique and wonderful adventure and I heard **HIS VOICE** again!

He said out loud ...

"Favor comes with sacrifice and Great favor comes with Great sacrifice untowards God!"

That was an amazing , amazing day!

God spoke aloud to me!

This has been applied to my life again and again and has much power attached to it!

It has guided me and allowed for growth on my part. These words helped put the onus on **me** in times of seeking favor.

I've spoken it over many situations to many people.

<u>**Genesis 4:4**</u>

And Abel also brought an offering-fat portions from some of the firstborn of his flock. The Lord looked with **favor** on Abel and his offering.

I immediately wrote it down as I could remember and used it as the basis for my next sermon the following Sunday! There was one more but I could not write fast enough and it left my mind. I know that sounds bad, but I have come to realize that the voice of the Father, Holy Spirit, Jesus, is a NOW experience as God is outside of time.

For me, the best way to remember is to write it down immediately upon hearing, either aloud, in my spirit, or visually presented. I started taking a notebook and pen with me to bed every evening. I did not want to miss a thing. At this point I was feeling like the most special person on the earth.

He also spoke the word **"Enoch"** **out loud to me and** I immediately looked up Enoch and found.

Genesis 5:24
And **Enoch** walked with God; and he was not, for God took him.

Hebrews 11:5

By faith **Enoch** was taken away so that he did not see death, and was not found, because God had taken him; for before he was taken he had this testimony, that he pleased God.

Powerful! I wanted to learn everything about God.

To read ALL I could get my hands on became my mission and I watched many evangelists and prophets on tv and online. I started to receive discernment on what/who was true and good and also who was not.

Book after book, I could not absorb enough about my new found gift.

Don't ignore your gifts. God wants you to have them. Pray for them.

He loves giving gifts.

Key take away #4   His words carry power. Use them.

Chapter 5   **The Chuckle**

Visiting my son's home, it got late and I decided to stay the night in his guest room for that evening.

He managed a club at that time and had a place to sleep where you would be comfortable to sleep if you stayed up until the club closed. His guest room is small and painted dark so that musicians that get in late are able to sleep through the morning after playing late into the night.

I was praying before turning in and what seemed like minutes turned out to be three or more hours of prayer. When I looked at the clock I was shocked that I had prayed so long while being so tired.

I said, "Lord I can't believe that we talked this long can you?" Just as clear as a bell I heard an out loud chuckle! It was wonderful.

I heard it as loud as if He was right beside me.

There is the kicker, he WAS right beside me.

Jesus is beside each of us ALL the time.

My confidence was building. I was emboldened! The Lord was really building me up. I was so encouraged about what he was telling me, when spoken to others it was coming to pass.

It was with much anxiety that I was preparing to go to SanFrancisco to an evangelism event by myself. Praying about it I heard the following in my spirit.

"Witherest thou goest, I'll be there."

This allowed me to realize I was not by myself at all and to calm down.

San Francisco physically alone still seemed pretty scary. I had made arrangements but had a touch of misgivings. I did however have my plane tickets purchased.

I had no other arrangements. I heard Gods words and pretty soon, all fell into place. I ended up staying with friends Mary Sybisma and Frances Brower and my room became available without cost as did my ride to and from the event. I met new friends and the whole of the event went well.

"Witherest thou goest I'll be there" When I heard these words spoken in my spirit, the use of the very old english was comforting. They were so quietly spoken in my spirit! Quiet, yet so reassuring. I knew I was not alone and felt very safe traveling with only the appearance of being alone. I was to shortly leave for home. All went well.

Joshua 1:9

Have I not command thee? Be strong and of good courage ; be not afraid, neither be thou dismayed: for the Lord thy God is with thee whithersoever thou goest.

Key takeaway #5

You are never alone when you have Jesus. He also has a sense of humor.

Chapter 6   **The Wishes**

One night, I was lying in bed in a room with two other ladies bunking at a camp. As far as I knew all were asleep except me. It was very early morning and I was praying silently while lying in bed before getting up for the day.

If I recall it correctly, I believe I was going down a list and trying to think of literally everything I could be thankful for and thanking **HIM** for all of it. All of a sudden in mid prayer I heard a **VOICE** say

"I will give you four things you wish for" and simultaneously, I saw a large gate open before my eyes. Tall curved center tapering to not as tall on each end. It opened in the middle before me, translucent white in color it was amazing.

I figured everyone must have heard and seen it and I looked to see.

Surprised to see they were all still asleep I laid back to try and understand all this.

I thought about it and kept on praying and told the Lord that was beautiful and felt like I wanted to be very careful with what I would request. I looked up some things in the Bible and proceeded with my wishes. Although they are very private, I must say my wishes were in compound sentences. I have every confidence that each thing I asked is on its way. I have already received a portion!

What an amazing God!

Chronicles 1 v 7-12

7 On that night God appeared to Solomon, and said to him, "Ask! What shall I give you?"

8 And Solomon said to God: "You have shown great mercy to David my father, and have made me king in his place. 9 Now, O LORD God, let Your promise to David my father be established, for You have made me king over a people like the dust of the earth in multitude. 10 Now give me wisdom and knowledge, that I may go out and come in before this people; for who can judge this great people of Yours?"

11 Then God said to Solomon: "Because this was in your heart, and you have not asked riches or wealth or honor or the life of your enemies, nor have you asked long life—but have asked wisdom and knowledge for yourself, that you may judge My people over whom I have made you king— 12 wisdom and knowledge are granted to you; and I will give you riches and wealth and honor, such as none of the kings have had who were before you, nor shall any after you have the like.

Key take away #6 God wants GREAT things for us!

Chapter 7   **The Alarm**

The next day I was to arise earlier than the others in the camp, at 6:00 AM but did not bring an alarm or my phone as they were not allowed.

I was to get up very early and go to a flea market and set up. All I could do was pray. I asked God to please help me awaken and not let me oversleep!

PLEASE! PLEASE! PLEASE!

I awakened the next day dreamily to a beautiful soft rain outside. So relaxed was I, that I completely forgot I was to get up early. I decided to go back to sleep. It was that beautiful kind of relaxing rain that you just melt together with it right into your bed.

Just then a lightning/thunder crash!!! happened right out my window. I mean **RIGHT** out my window. I mean it sounded like it split the wall/window right by my bed!

Well, it was 6:00 AM right on the dot. God has great timing and a beautiful sense of humor. I got up feeling so special to have Dad wake me up himself.

I looked around the room only to find it had not phased a soul. No one had even stirred. It was as if I was the only one who heard it. God has sooooo many kids. I felt very loved and punctual.

Zechariah 4:1

And the angel that talked with me came again and waked me, as a man that is awakened out of his sleep.

He loves each one of us AND wants to spend eternity with each of us. Do you share your day with HIM? He wants to share it with YOU!

Key take away #7   God is interested in even the smallest of our details. God is always on time.

Chapter 8   **The Amethyst**

That night I had a vision of an Amethyst colored gem and the words "look it up" "look it up" were spoken into my spirit.

I did not take time to look it up though, as I had to get going and set up at a flea market that day. I was in the truck with my business partner (future husband), Gary who is co-pastor at the church I preach at. We were driving back from Des Moines and I was telling him about the amethyst vision. While we were talking about it I asked if he knew what it meant off the top of his head.

He did not, but while that conversation was happening, Gary got a random call from a friend who was coming in from California to do the same flea market with us. We had not heard from him in a year or more. He told Gary that he had something I might like and could he (Gary) hand me the phone.

Well, when he got me on the phone he said had I ever seen an **amethyst**?

Well, that got my attention and I said I was very interested in seeing what he had. I asked many questions but he said

"Sheri,This is what you are to do. Look 'em up, look 'em up."

Oh my goodness he just used the exact same words that had been spoken to me the night before.

Well, I did look it up and found that in the bible the amethyst is considered the dream stone, and is also connected with royalty.

When Jim (the man with the large amethysts) got to the market from California, he walked across the fairgrounds and handed me one of these beautiful stones and told me he did not know why he was so compelled to see that I got one, but here it is. He just felt he was to see that I got one.

Wow! I felt like God sent me a gift special delivery.

Oh yes God is great! He speaks to you, but you have to seek him.

Scripture Exodus 28:19

The third row was jacinth, agate, and a purple amethyst

I found that Aaron the prophet/high priest was to wear Amethyst as one of the gems to be worn in remembrance of the tribes of Israel on his breastplate.

Key takeaway #8   God holds us in high esteem.

Chapter 9   A moving prayer

I was on my way to an appointment that was in a town an hour and a half from my home, Des Moines. It was an important appointment and honestly its contents and agenda had consumed my mind. I started driving and was kind of running the conversation that I imagined would happen at my appointment over and over through my mind. In all this concentration on all the what could be's of my pending meeting, I was about a mile from my destination and I ran out of gas at a stop sign.

Now this could have thrown me out of getting to the meeting all together and THEN IT OCCURRED TO ME TO PRAY!

When I stalled, I was at an intersection at the bottom of a hill. I then needed to make a turn from a standstill position, go up a hill, take a right, go a bit, turn right into a gas station, and again into the pump. Impossible, from a stationary position , unable to start my car at the bottom of the hill.

I prayed!

The light turned green, and my car started to coast thru the intersection, (remember I was stalled to a complete stop at the bottom of a hill and out of gas). (My engine was OFF) Slowly, I began to gain, the kind of speed you pick up when coasting down a hill. The only difference was **I was turning and going UP a hill**. I then kept coasting, going right around the corner, right into the gas station and then another right to the pump and then it came to a complete stop. Right at the only open pump.

There is no way that I can think of that this could have happened. Not one plausible way that this occurred without prayer and God supernaturally sending angels unseen to take a car from a complete stop, push it up a hill, and continue to push it through until it reached the required destination.

I thanked God mightily for the push, pumped and paid for my gas, started up my car and proceeded to the meeting God would have me attend on time. He is so good and with you always.

Psalm 103:20

Bless the Lord, ye his angels, that excel in strength, that do his commandments, hearkening unto the voice of his word.

Mark 10:27

Jesus looked at them and said," With men this is impossible but with God all things are possible."

Key take away #9 God can send an army of angels and make ALL things possible.

Chapter 10   The Cross

On another morning, we were having a church service. It was a rainy morning around 11:00 AM and things in the service were just about to get started. A man named Bob and I were taking apart the lighted cross at the front of the altar, sliding out the glass panels on the front to get to the burned out light bulbs. All the light bulbs were burned out and had that blackened area on them that happens when burned out except for one bulb still working at the bottom of the cross. We took out all the bulbs that were burnt out and blackened except the one that worked at the bottom, vowed to replace the others by the following Sunday, shook each one and heard the little filament rattle. We then replaced the bulbs and put back the glass to the front of the cross so that we could proceed to have church. We turned on what would light and proceeded to get ready for church with our one bulb cross that was dark on the whole thing except for one Christmas size lightbulb at the very bottom that was not burned out.

Our church is a small congregation of hungry for the Lord believers, set in the setting of an old storefront church conversion on the main street of a small town. At the front of the church is a pulpit and behind and above the pulpit is the cross I mentioned that lights up as the focal point of the altar. Anyway that said , it was starting to storm.

There was a lot of, thunder, rumbling and lightning.

All of a sudden there was a loud clap of lightning and thunder and **ALL the electricity went out at once**. Well, there we all sat, all dressed up and ready to worship God and **the lights went out.**

Now I am co pastors in the church with Pastor Gary Smith. He preaches in the morning and I preach Sunday night. We have a full day of church and a full body of believers that come to spend the ENTIRE day

When the lights went out, there was no air conditioning and no lights in the whole church.

Gary asked the congregation at that point what they wanted to do? Go on and have church with the electric off? Or dismiss until the next week?

As if orchestrated by a director, the congregation said at once,

"Have Church".

All of a sudden, in sync with that answer, the cross turned on.

The CROSS TURNED ON!

ALL the lights in the cross turned on!

Now you might not think that unusual because electricity often comes back on in a storm after going out, BUT THIS WAS UNUSUAL.

All the bulbs had been off but one and now ALL the lights of the cross were on!!!

The electricity had not come back on.

One of the people in our congregation that day was a licensed electrician. No other power was available in that church except God's almighty power!

The transformer had been knocked out for the whole town and no power was naturally coming into the building. You could plug it in or unplug it the lights were on either way.

Well, God got a standing ovation on that one and we had quite a day celebrating Him. I also should add that when God powers the cross it does not matter whether or not the bulbs are burned out or not. They all came on. We all took out our cell phones and took pictures of our little burned out cross burning brightly with ALL its bulbs in the middle of a storm that the other churches in the town decided to go home and dismiss, when the power went out city wide. It was great and so was church that day.

When the power came back on the cross went back to one bulb illumination.

God is so amazing!

Psalm 68:35

God is awesome in his sanctuary. The God of Israel gives power and strength to his people. Praise be to God.

Zechariah 4:6

So he said to me,"This is the word of the Lord to Zerubbabel: Not by might, nor by power, but by my Spirit ; says the Lord Almighty

Key take away #10 God does not limit us and can give us power.

Chapter 11   The storm got worse!

Six days a week I work as a picker, along side the other pastor at the church discovering unique finds in barns, attics, factory warehouses, etc. When we don't have a client at one of our nine warehouses, we travel 250 miles a day seeking out great finds and being blessed with at least a truckload a day. In fact we make it a policy to not come home unless we have a truckload and we always come home.

A tornado came through the area and several buildings were destroyed. Many barns were completely wiped out. Earlier that day we prayed for protection for our warehouses . We rent the land for the biggest of our barns we own. It is chock full of product and was completely unprotected without the prayer. We were not insured by man.

Anyway, as we said, many barns in the area were completely destroyed and in that specific area ALL the out buildings were affected in some way or another EXCEPT ours! Now what makes that so amazing is that our barn sits in between two other barns. One of them is so close to ours it is connected by a 10 foot hallway.

Both barns on either side were destroyed. The one that was connected was **completely destroyed except for the hallway that connected theirs to ours. Our barn was completely saved**.

Our other buildings were completely protected. Not a shingle or sheet of tin was disturbed yet the power poles across the road and on the same side were sheared off at the base. We felt blessed, blessed !

Blessed, Blessed, Blessed.

Psalm 41:2

The Lord will protect and preserve them. They are counted among the blessed in the land. He does not give them over to the desires of their foes. The Lord He will bless him in the land.

Key take away #11   The Lord wants to bless us!

Chapter 12　　　**The Lights**

Now the lights to our building were another thing. The power poles to the destroyed building were sheared off at the base as was the building that the poles powered. That left us as the connecting building without power. We were not in a position to ask for it to be repaired, as the building the power went out in was also destroyed. We kept quiet on the subject as we pay nothing for power and it had been a pure gift in the past.

I said it would cost thousands to bring power to just our building and we were just going to be without. That was that.

The man that owned the property had sustained such damage that it would have been ridiculous for us to bring up our loss of electricity to him at all AND even if we had, had the guts to be so bold it would have required him to spend way too much to bring the electric to just our building, so we just decided to suck it up and be content with what little light we had that came through the skylights into our building.

Customers came and customers went and we thought about the lights no more. Somehow we were working our schedule so that we got our best light when we were in that building. God just kept blessing us with a schedule allowing us to work around not having any lights

But one night I had a vision of a barn that I recognized to be a small building /barn by the house of the man that owned the farm that our building was on.

What made the vision unique was that the building had lights brightly streaming from every crack , door and window of the small barn by his house. I got to wondering what it represented? Blessings? Illumination on blessings?

We, (Gary and a guy who worked for us that day and myself) were all driving down the highway and I was discussing this with them. We were within a mile of the property when a lightbulb went off in my head and I exclaimed out loud...

"What if?"

"Just what if? That vision meant that the property owner had gone to the trouble of restoring our ability to have power and God just wanted us to know about it."

Well as I recall no one in the truck thought that was likely and I said, "We are so close can we just check? Please?"

That was not our destination, so this was not a popular idea because it would seem I was just going to make us late by this supposed folly. Well, we went there and I asked Gary if he would go up the ramp to the barn and flip the switch.

He did not think it worthy at that moment, so I went up the ramp and hit the switch right inside the door.

(DRUM ROLL PLEASE)

The lights came on and had been restored that very day.

Glory! What a friend God is! His Holy Spirit gave us a tip to flip a switch we would NEVER have flipped ever again.

It was so beautiful and we all stopped at that moment and gave thanks to a Father that loves us so much that no detail is too small for Him. Praise you Lord ! Thank you so much!

Luke 12:6

Are not five sparrows sold for two farthings, and not one of them is forgotten before God?

Key take away #12 God, is interested in every detail.

Chapter 13   Creation of Light Vision

I have found that one word or picture from the Lord holds an amazing amount of power. It can build you up more than anything that I can think of.

One night, I was awake but in bed. With eyes wide open in the darkest of dark nights I saw the word Void sear through the darkness with the letters scorched thru by streaming light.

The night was pitch dark as was all the surrounding area except for the hugely bright searing light cutting through the darkness! It spelled the word VOID!It was an amazing lesson!He showed me how He created light through His spoken word by speaking into the darkness in the void of the night.

Genesis 1:3

And God said "Let there be light,"and there was light

Key Take away #13 He wants us to know and to see.

Chapter 14   **The Christmas Sale**

It was Christmas time and our ministry gives out
Christmas presents to as many kids as we can find in
need. Some with hard circumstances, incarcerated
parents and not much hope of having a good
Christmas. We were so blessed from God to give out so
many presents but between Gary and me, shopping,
wrapping and delivering that year, it seems I had let
my own home go a shambles and it was only three
days before Christmas.

I didn't even have my tree up. My son was coming
home the next day and I wasn't ready for my own
family's Christmas. In fact, we had done so much
getting ready for everyone else's Christmas that
coming into the holiday with only three days left I was
just exhausted.

We were to carol that night and we still had a few more
deliveries of gifts to go. I started to cry, overwhelmed
by the imbalance of the tasks ahead.

It was already Christmas Eves' eve and we (Gary and
I) were on our way to town to deliver the last of the
presents and I asked him if he minded if I just shut my
eyes just a few moments to rest ? He said of course and
I immediately fell asleep and dreamed.

All of a sudden I was awakened out of this sleep by my own dream and was wide awake.

An excited voice said... as if in a commercial **"and now for three days only, three days only take 100% off yes that's right 100% off."**

"Now through Christmas take 100% off, 100% off,"

Wide awake I immediately and excitedly turned to Gary and said, "Gary the Lord just gave me three days off until Christmas. He just wants me to quit work and go home and get ready for my Christmas."

No sooner than I said that, I got a call from my son Steven, from his city two hours away and because of the weather he was coming in a day early.

I said, "Well Steve, I don't have to carol tonight, I have the night off, let's put up the tree together and have a good evening!"

The Lord is so wonderful.

After we had distributed all the presents and with my son safely home as I lay in bed that night it felt so good as we had given out over 900 presents. Pretty good from a church that only owned three cars between all of us.

"Dear Lord, it was so wonderful,"I prayed.

"I thank you for all the things that you allowed us to do, for you provided everything!"

"Lord I thank you so much!" and as I was praying that prayer, I saw a man at the end of my bed. HE LOOKED at me and smiled the biggest smile. He was so beautiful, He was wearing a brown tweed coat and his pockets were pulled out of his pants as if to show that he had nothing. I believe that he represented the people that we gave the presents to.

I don't know if it was the Lord or an angel.

I started to speak to Him and just as I started to speak I noticed His eyes were so beautiful and His smile was so big.

I got to the part of thanking Him and just then my daughter Sally burst into my room and said "Mom you will never believe what Matt just texted me" and just like that He disappeared!

I won't forget, you know, He was so beautiful, He seemed so pleased and He looked at me as just a job well done. I looked at the place in the room from where He was standing and it really would've been impossible for Him to stand there because there was a pile of blankets that were where His feet were. I guess in reality He was in the spirit world where all things are possible.

I did see Him.

I was not frightened

 AND

He did look pleased!

Mathew 25:40

Then shall he answer them, saying verilyI say unto you, Inasmuch as ye have done unto one of the least of these my brethren, ye have done it to me.

I was pleased too.

Key Take Away #14 Thanking Him goes two ways.

48

Chapter 15   **The Parking space**

I don't think that you can ever be thankful enough for all the things that God provides us on a day to day basis. It is amazing how many details that God covers for us. One thing I have come to realize is the more you are thankful for, the more you will have from the smallest detail on.

I had broken my ankle and Gary and I were going to the store. In my minds voice I prayed for a parking spot that would allow me to go into the store without the trouble created for everyone involved that comes from a long walk.

Just as I opened my eyes, a place unexpectedly opened up for us to park that was right by the door.

We started thanking the Lord for a parking place every time we needed and the funny thing was we always got a good spot. We just kept thanking Him for such seemingly small things and He just kept blessing us with those parking spaces and bigger and bigger things.

God is in the details and worthy to be praised. He is our best friend. I thank Him for every small detail He attends.

You know you can pray like He is your best friend because He is.

Do you thank him for the seemingly small things?

Do not just pray when in trouble. Thank Him, thank Him, thank Him!

Mathew 10:29

Are not two sparrows sold for a penny? Yet not one of them will fall to the ground outside your Father's care.

Key take away #15   Oh how He loves us.

Chapter 16   The Music

I had been writing this book and was full of God when I went to bed on that evening. I said a prayer and I really cannot tell you what it was about, but the point is that I felt so full of the spirit. I felt really close to God.

Anyway...that morning about 5:30 in the morning I was awakened by a chorus in my spirit that was singing. Oh what a Beautiful morning ...Oh What a beautiful day!

It truly was and I was so grateful for the opportunity to wake up so in his presence. He sent a choir of angels. Beautiful!

Psalm 28:7

The Lord is my strength and my shield; my heart trusts in Him, and helps me. My heart leaps for joy and with my song I praise him.

Key take away #16   The Joy of the Lord is my strength.

Chapter 17   **The Tree**

One night church was going great. It was one of those nights where everyone was really into worship and no one was watching the clock. Everyone was just praising God. All of a sudden in the middle of a prayer, the tree in the corner of the room started to strongly shake. It kept shaking and shaking.

Now let me set this up. There were no open windows for a wind. No air conditioner blowing, no furnace blowing, we opened the front door, all was still outside. It was on a concrete floor which was still.

It was a move of God. Something only explainable if attributed to God.

Psalm 96:12

Let the field be jubilant, and everything in them; let all the trees of the forest sing for joy.

Key take away #17 God can give joy even to trees.

Chapter 18 The Radio

I love this story if for no other reason than to show the depth of Gods love.

It was a snowy night and my youngest son Steven had just left my house on Christmas vacations end. I went to bed with a great deal of worry about the roads. I prayed for his safe trip to his home. It was a two hour drive for him and the roads were not too good. You would have called it a blizzard. Eventually, I must have drifted off to sleep.

I awakened to the sounds of cheers at a baseball game on the radio and Jack Bucks' voice (voice of the St. Louis Cardinals for years) yelled, "heeeeeeeeeeeeeeeeee's safe." The radio then turned off.

Thinking about this I had to chuckle when I realized, **I had no radio**. He just let this old Cardinals fan and former softball fanatic know her son had just gotten home safe! I called my son immediately and confirmed it was true. He had just walked in the door! Beautiful!

What a friend we have in Jesus!

John 14:16

And I will pray the Father, and He will give you another Helper, that He may abide with you forever.

Key take away #18   When God is for you, who can be against you.

Chapter 19 The Shoves

There was one night I was lying in bed and someone shoved me on my shoulder while I was sleeping. It awakened me and I, annoyed said, "Stop it."

I got shoved again on my left shoulder as I was lying on my right side. I pulled my covers up closer and was even more determined to sleep on.

One more time I was shoved and I finally said, "What?" As I awakened, I realized that there was NO ONE in the room to have shoved me BUT as I became even more aware, a dream came flooding back to me that was later very important to me.

I was now awake enough to take my pen and pad of paper that I take to bed with me and write down the dream. In my most quiet times is when I hear from the Lord and do not want to ever miss anything again!

I believe an angel awakened me so that I would be aware enough to actually receive that important dream message.

I was so grateful!

Zechariah 4:1

Now the angel who talked with me came back and wakened me, as a man who is wakened out of his sleep.

Key take away #19   Angels are messengers and you are not to sleep through the message.

Chapter 20   One with the Word

One night my husband Gary and I were at a very spirit filled church service. At this time, Evangelist and Pastor Richard Schlotter was bringing home the WORD as only he can. About a third of the way into his message his voice became that of running water and his body became transparent as the WORD was delivered. He also for a brief time seemed to ascend in the air as he spoke. I could understand everything he was saying but it was as if he at that moment had become one with the word.

I mention this because it was just another way that God, The Holy Spirit, Jesus shows himself.

I have seen similar things with other evangelists particularly once when evangelist Chris Owensby was coming up the aisle of a church he was excitedly speaking at while bringing the word in Holy Spirit style. He seemed to transcend time for a brief period and become transparent and elevated in the air while preaching. These are great times to be alive.

The WORD of God is ALIVE, and beautiful to behold.

Ezekiel 43:2
And behold, the glory of the God of Israel came from the way of the East. His voice *was* like the sound of many waters; and the earth shone with His glory.

John 1
Eternal word
1 In the beginning was the Word, and the Word was with God, and the Word was God.

Key take away #20   The Holy Spirit that lives within and the Word are One.

Chapter 21   The Angel

I heard an angel speak to me and the last part of what it said was spoken in the voice of Ronald Reagan. The angel said to go to Washington DC and meet them at the center of the mall. It also told me these are the folks you should be hanging around with. I didn't know what that meant but I was excited to be obedient.

I also had a vision of Benny Hinn laying hands on my head while I was on a set of five stairs.

That week I was invited to Washington DC so I got an airplane ticket. Benny Hinn was in Washington DC that week and I was not working this event. None of the crew I worked most closely with at the Benny Hinn events were working this particular event.

So I decided to put God's request together with this trip. Have you ever realized how well things work when you are walking in the Spirit, so to speak.

The Lord really works with you when you are obedient to His will. But what was the why of His will? I was really confused.

I was on a plane for a Benny Hinn event in Washington DC. and that was my only clue. The other thing I knew was that He had sent a messenger to speak to me to meet Him in the mall, in the center of the mall in Washington DC.

I had, had the privilege to go to many of the Benny Hinn events that year and work as part of their ministry. I believe that going to those events actually was instrumental in stretching my belief system to be open to more and more from God. Going to events where people are healed in an atmosphere of pure worship was very revealing to me.

A lot happens when you worship. God inhabits your worship. You lose your sense of self in true worship. You surrender. It is wonderful. I feel it is key.

Some things are difficult to discern but when you see people that are deaf hear for the first time. You start believing real fast.

Well, I wanted to put my all into this trip and decided to put in a twenty-one day fast for its success and had the fast end simultaneously with the crusades start. I had just enough time.

I dedicated the fast to God. All I said was "Lord, I am going to do this for you and I would love to have a good seat at the event. May I?"

Well, I went to the airport to check into my flight and found I was too late and I missed my flight.

I was too late without being too late.

Hmmm.

I was thinking seriously? If God wanted me to go on this journey how did this happen?

That was Thursday and the event started on Thursday at 7PM. I asked if they had more flights for DC available that day. They said they did but it would cost me $50 to change to the next flight which was to get in after 5PM Washington, DC time. Well, that was it, I bought a book (Psalms 91), I got on the flight and settled into my seat.

Seated on each side of me I felt was a different end of the spectrum in beliefs. It was just an assumption based on actions and appearances. Flanked to my left was what appeared to be a small lady from India with a colorful scarf around her head, beautiful olive skin and a warm, vibrant smile. That was my left side.

To my right, was a woman who dressed as if she had great means, that seemed rather put out that she had to be seated by either of us, the Indian lady or I.

She immediately made it fairly clear that by not returning our greetings she was not interested in speaking to either of us and immediately buried her head in a book!

I smiled at the little Indian lady, shut my eyes, laid back my head and immediately pondered the Lord's directions to me.

1. I was told to go to Washington DC.

2. In a vision I had seen Benny Hinn walk up to me and lay hands on my head. (Having been to and worked as staff at many of his events already and knowing they don't quite roll that way with security and all, I didn't quite know what that meant.)

3. In Ronald Reagen's voice I heard "Now these are the kind of people you should associate with!"

4. Also I had heard the words to meet Him in the mall ,in the middle of the mall.

Well, I did not have a clue at that point of my journey what any of it meant but I laid back to ponder just that!

 What did it mean?

All of a sudden I opened my eyes and looked at the woman reading beside me. I had the most compelling urge to ask her about what the 4th thing, (what the mall thing) meant.

As I looked at her she seemed very contently reading a mystery novel but the urge seemed great, so I interrupted her.

"Excuse me," I said. "Do you live in Washington DC?" I asked.

Looking over her reading glasses she gave me a look that could have/should have turned me to ice. Not to be dissuaded (this urge was great) I proceeded.

"Excuse me, If someone you were to meet asked you to 'meet them at the mall, in the center of the mall, what would that mean to you?' She looked me right in the eye and said 'That is easy"

She then, extended her left arm straight forward and said, "At the peek of my finger tips is the Lincoln Memorial, at my elbow is the US Capital. The White House is up and right of my wrist, and the Jefferson Memorial is to the left of my wrist. You see it is all built in the shape of a cross. They want to meet you at the center of the cross."

She then without further ado immediately went back to her book and to my amazement, God had used this woman, seemingly unknowingly, to tell me He wanted to meet me at the cross. That I should come to Him at the cross. I was so excited. As I pondered that revelation I wondered what else my dear Lord had in store for me on this trip.

The plane landed sometime after 5:30 and the event was at a church, in a suburb. A church can only hold so many people, so I was starting to be very concerned about the wisdom of my adventure.

That thought was soon erased by the excitement of the possibilities of the evening and I settled into a cab and watched as the driver drove. I got a taxi and by 6:45 we were seemingly lost and I was starting to doubt if I was going to get to any event at all.

We pulled into a McDonalds parking lot in the DC suburb of the event and seemed to be circling it time and time again.

Ok, that was enough!

The cab driver was running a tab at my expense. He said he was lost and I suggested the church was not to be found in the McDonalds parking lot!

I began to pray. "Lord please help me get to the event, I Love you so much!" No more had I said that, than a rather large, (VERY LARGE) dark man came out of a car (blue Volkswagen bug) and started walking briskly toward my car window. For reasons that make no sense whatsoever, I started hesitantly to crack the windowand he said hurriedly, "Are you going to the Benny Hinn Event?"

I said "Yes" and he said, "Pull out of this drive, turn left, then take a right and at the top of the hill go left again and the church will be on your left."

I said "Thanks," rolled up the window and thought "Did that really just happen? Was that a man or a messenger from God?"

I was blown away but no sooner had I completed that thought when I arrived at the church.

THE LINE WAS HUGE! No, it was actually bigger than that!

I paid the driver, walked past the line, passing the front of it and went to a desk and asked if there was any pastor seating available? She looked at me as if "Are you kidding?"

She said, "We have 2000 more people here than we can seat and it is 7:00 already." She said I would have to go to the end of the line but would not likely get a seat as they were filled past where the fire marshal's capacity number would allow already.

Just then a nicely dressed girl walked up to me and asked if I was with the Benny Hinn group.

I said "no"

"Follow me!" she said.

I asked if she was from Benny Hinn's group (as she was quite smartly dressed) and she said, "No" and we started walking down the aisle of the huge church.

What was happening? The line outside was wrapped around the block, waiting to get in to an event that was already 2,000 people over capacity.

This church was a buzz with excitement and filled to the brim. She was walking quickly and we had soon passed the cheap seats.

Walking further down the aisle we passed the ordinary seats. I looked to my right while briskly walking and saw my friends Mary and Frances whom I was sure had been there for hours to get those seats.

"Oh my God" I thought, "You are giving me a good seat! Thank you! Thank you! Thank you!" and then I realized that I was even passing the VIP's.

Ok, now I was in front row, passing the right of the stage as you face it. I couldn't believe it, I was in the front row past the center, at the right of the stage as you face it.

I said thank you to God and jokingly said to God "What no center seats available?"

That thought was interrupted by a lady who asked if I would give up my seat to a man that was being held up by a person on each side of him who could not walk.

 I said, "Of course."

He could not stand on his own and they helped him all the way to the seat. Then the first lady came to me and said once again "Follow me". She started on the stage and I stood at the bottom of the stage and waited at the base of the stage for her return.

She turned to me and said

"Follow me."

"On the stage?"

"Yes," she said. I followed her and she sat me right in the front row on the stage exactly in the middle.

Right behind where Benny Hinn would speak.

I sat by an excitable young pastor from Iran, who kept calling me mama. "Aren't we blessed mama?" he said patting my knee repeatedly.

"Aren't we blessed Mama?" He said again patting my knee.

If you have ever been to a Benny Hinn event you know the power and presence of the Lord arrives amidst the worship of thousands and He never seems to disappoint. One of the hardest working evangelists alive, Pastor Hinn is completely in tune with the Holy Spirit and knows that when the time is right that literally "All things are possible." Putting it another way, God shows up and things happen.

Benny Hinn then came on the stage, turned from the crowd in the audience to face us on the stage, and said he was going to do something special and lay hands and anoint the pastors on the stage. He asked us to line up as God had asked him to pass on a prophetic healing mantel.

My mind was whirling, this was like in my vision, but I had been to so many of these events that I knew this not to be the norm. We stood up from our seats and formed a short line.

"Aren't we blessed mama?" said the Iranian pastor "Aren't we blessed? "

Indeed I was.

The anointing was so strong on Pastor Hinn that I was having a hard time standing as I got close. Somehow the line held me up and Pastor Hinn laid hands on me and passed the anointing, blessing.

When I came around and we were through the line we started running and laying hands on everyone. We were running hand in hand in joy and laying hands on all who would allow it, the Iranian Pastor and myself. The anointing was there and I now understood three of the things told to me about the trip.

1. Go to DC (check...obedience)

2. Meet Him at the mall (the mall meant cross and if you are willing to seek the mysteries of God, He will show himself to you in beautiful ways.)

3.When I saw the vision of my head being anointed by Pastor Hinn I could not perceive the reality that it could even be possible. I could not perceive being singled out in a crowd of 10,000 people. It was true Benny Hinn actually anointed me. I was anointed by Benny Hinn but I did not understand the

4th word that was told to me with Ronald Reagans voice, that said "These are the kind of people you should be associating with."

A gal who I had worked with in the Hinn group named June Touismo called across the church for me and offered me a ride.It turns out there were no cabs available to the area after eight.

"What are the odds?" I thought. "No cabs are available after eight in that area." yet I got a ride on the Benny Hinn bus, to their hotel. My plane was to return home yet that night so I hopped another ride to the airport with a couple from June's hotel. I had been rerouted so many times that it turned out that I ended up flying in AND flying out same day.

I looked at my ticket that had been reissued and could not believe it. To get me home the airline had rerouted my flight to Ronald Reagan Airport. On the way to the event I had been reading a book I was drawn to at the airport in Des Moines called

Psalm 91 which says__

1 He who dwells in the secret place of the Most High
Shall abide under the shadow of the Almighty.

2 I will say of the Lord, "He is my refuge and my fortress;
My God, in Him I will trust."
3 Surely He shall deliver you from the snare of the fowler
And from the perilous pestilence.
4 He shall cover you with **His feathers**,
And under His wings you shall take refuge;
His truth shall be your shield and buckler.
5 You shall not be afraid of the terror by night,
Nor of the arrow that flies by day,
6 Nor of the pestilence that walks in darkness,
Nor of the destruction that lays waste at noonday.
7 A thousand may fall at your side,
And ten thousand at your right hand;
But it shall not come near you.

8 Only with your eyes shall you look,

And see the reward of the wicked.

9 Because you have made the Lord, who is my refuge,

Even the Most High, your dwelling place,

10 No evil shall befall you,

Nor shall any plague come near your dwelling;

11 For He shall give His angels charge over you,

To keep you in all your ways.

12 In their hands they shall bear you up,

Lest you dash your foot against a stone.

13 You shall tread upon the lion and the cobra,

The young lion and the serpent you shall trample underfoot.

14 "Because he has set his love upon Me, therefore I will deliver him;

I will set him on high, because he has known My name.

15 He shall call upon Me, and I will answer him;

I will be with him in trouble;

I will deliver him and honor him.

16 With long life I will satisfy him."

I had actually finished the book on the flight.

I got to the airport and it was very clean and shiny. Super shiny! Granite floors and stainless steel.

My flight was to leave in the wee hours before sun up...and thinking about all that had happened, laying on the floor, I drifted off to sleep with my bag under my head and my black vest was thrown over me.

Pretty soon a group of people were chattering beside me and I looked up to see a person standing over me saying, "are you to take this flight?" Looking up at them from the airport floor I dazedly looked around and realized the answer was "yes."

People were getting in line and I turned to thank the person but they were no where to be found! Angel? I cannot say for a fact, I do know when I got in line, I realized I was in the midst of several people from the Benny Hinn Event, that travel as part of the entourage that I worked with. I got in line and a lady said. "She is with us!" We are the people she is to be associating with."

Wow! Now I knew I was on track and God had been with me every step of the way.

Did I mention My black vest had tiny white feathers stuck in the fabric of my vest, **quill part out, feather part in**?

Strange? YES!

God? YES!

Now each instruction God gave me on this adventure made sense and The night was wonderful and I came home having fulfilled each item of instruction from the Lord…

getting Anointed and Blessed and also had a

VERY good seat!

Key take away #21   God has a very special place and purpose for those who listen.

Chapter 23   The Healing

One night I was sleeping and had a vision of a girl that came to our church. Her name was Karla. The vision was kind of strange in that it showed Karla with an extended tummy, much like a pregnant girl checking out at a store. As quickly as I saw it, it was gone.

What did it mean? I was not sure so I thought about it , pondered it and prayed. Soon after that my friend I was with got a call.

"Oh no," he said. "They just found Karla in her room." This was a Monday. She hasn't eaten or drank anything since Friday.

She was too weak to get out of bed, to use the toilet, get a drink or eat. She was too weak to answer her phone. They say she is unresponsive, in a coma and not expected to live the night.

I then knew what the message of my vision was. Karla was checking out, literally checking out and I believe it had something to do by reason of her abdomen.

We went to the hospital immediately and we were told she would not recover nor live through the night. We were also told she could not have anyone in her room. SO... we prayed in the hall. We prayed big, we prayed hard.

She lived throughout the night.

What happened next, the doctors were stunned. Well, many tests were to follow and they found she had cancer down in that area, the abdominal had been exaggerated in the vision.

They had to strengthen her up prior to her cancer surgery but ....oh, yeah, you are way ahead of me.

She is cancer free and giving her testimony to all who will hear.

Exodus 23:25

25 "So you shall serve the Lord your God, and He will bless your bread and your water. And I will take sickness away from the midst of you."

Key take away #22.   God gives visions so we may pray to activate His Word, Will and Way.

Chapter 23   **The Piano**

Have you ever been so in love with God that you just cannot get enough of worship?

That was the mood I was in that November and I started going to any and all services that would open their doors to me. One night I was sitting with several friends and we were sitting down to the left of the stage right beside the bench of the keyboard player. She was directing the music as she had written it and at one point got up to go over to the guitar player and correct his chord progression. As she got up to correct the guitar player, the piano kept playing.

Puzzled we looked at each other. The piano played ever so softly just a few notes, but oh so sweetly. As she walked back we excitedly told her what had happened.

She looked at us kind of funny and said "Well, we all know that is not possible," and sat down to continue to play. We just looked at each other and said it did happen. We did hear it! We all saw it and heard it and all things are possible with God.

Zephaniah 3:17

The Lord your God is in your midst, a mighty one who will save; He will rejoice over you with gladness; He will quiet you by His love; he will exalt over you with singing.

Key take away #23   He will rejoice over you with gladness, music and love.

Chapter 24   The Heart Surgery

One night I saw three visions that really gave me pause.

The first one was a right hand of a man, holding a scalpel and drawing it down the center of a chest and then the surgical line immediately disappeared.

The second vision was a picture of a beating heart, and at the top right side, the aorta seems to "BLING" like the British girls teeth in the gum commercial on TV.

The third thing was, I saw the word AUGURED spelled out and simultaneously out of my mouth I said. You spelled it wrong. (Correcting the Lord's spelling?)

Well, I am a woodworker and the word auger to me meant to bore or ream out as with a drill.

I immediately felt someone was going to have surgery on their heart and that the Lord had shown me that in doing so they were also going to need it reamed out, such as to clear a blockage.

That got me in prayer mode and I immediately thought of those closest to me.

Gary had suffered a heart attack in the past so I spoke with my friend and so as not to scare Gary, I asked the friend to pray with me for Gary.

I also went to Gary and as my friend had also had a previous heart attack and asked him to pray with me against any heart problem my friend might have.

That accomplished, I confidently went about my business and started planning an eventful weekend of shopping with my daughter in Iowa City. It was Friday and we were to leave Saturday morning around seven for our day.

Having my hair in curlers, so that I was presentable when my daughter arrived, I sat, seated on my sofa.

As I watched TV, I began the task of taking the curlers down with my arms overhead individually unrolling the curls, above my head. That's when it hit me.

My chest seemed to explode and it came on so swiftly and hard that I could neither call out to my roommate for help, nor could I stand to help myself.

With my hands still up on top of my head, from taking out the curlers, I do remember continuing my arms up to full extension. The next part I do not know if I said out loud or within myself but either way I spoke with the Lord.

"Thank you Lord, for the victory that will come of this for Your honor and glory. Thank you for showing me the surgery and the victory that will come from augering out the blockage."

At that point I tried to stand and collapsed to the floor.

It must have made quite a noise because my roommate had heard me fall from the other room and came on the run.

Since that is one of the persons I had spoken about that had, had a heart attack prior, he had nitroglycerin tablets on hand and placed a couple under my tongue.

He called Gary, (who lived next door and is now my husband) and he came over right away. They called an ambulance.

I passed out.

The next part that I remember is that they had me on a gurney in an ambulance heading for Iowa City an hour and a half away.

At this point I was still being given nitro tablets and being administered morphine, all the while taking constant measure of my blood pressure. I must have been in and out of consciousness as I only remember parts.

One thing I did know, was that I felt I knew I was not going to die, as God had shown me that I was going to have heart surgery and that it was going to heal quickly.

Also, I felt that I was possibly having surgery for clearing blockage and that is why I saw the word auger.

Whatever God had shown me gave me a huge calm as I knew He had shown me life.

Going fast in the ambulance, I remember vaguely hearing the EMT shout to the ambulance driver "We're losing her. Her blood pressure has dropped to 40/20."

He also shouted "she's non verbal"

Once again he shouted

"I'm losing her!"

Listening, somehow I did not get alarmed when he said he was losing me, because I thought… I haven't had my surgery yet and the Lord showed me that I would heal quickly after a surgery.

I did however, get stuck on the fact he said, "I was not verbal" and decided to check it out.

With all the strength I could muster I blurted "Do you know Jesus?"

At that moment he hollered to the driver and said, "She's back!" He then said, "not like you do" and he asked my level of pain, gave me more nitro and morphine.

By rides end, I had taken 9 nitros and had morphine continuously administered for pain. When we arrived at Iowa City, they had apparently called in my family as in the Doctors words to me, "It was bad."

Apparently I had enzymes in my liver, etc, they rolled me into a room to have some type of scan in a tube to see about surgery. Sorry that is not more technical of a description but I wasn't very coherent at that point.

The next part I remember VERY clearly, as a handsome, slim man , in a white coat, came in and said I was going to have my tests administered by him and that was unusual as he was not a tech but the doctor who would more than likely continue with any procedures going forward.

I said I already knew he was going to do surgery and asked how quickly my chest would heal.

He looked puzzled and said "Why do you ask? Why did you think you were going to have surgery? You did not know yet that I was your surgeon did you? "

I responded somewhat shyly about the real reason as I did not want to get reassigned to the mental ward. I even said as much.

He then looked me square in the eye and said, "Oh I am probably the only doctor in this place who would understand you." He said. "Well, you don't have to tell me but I will tell you that I am probably the only doctor in the place who had a little pentecostal grandmother that probably would have said the same thing to me."

I remember weakly smiling at him and then he proceeded to run the test going back and forth from me to an office and back to me.

He stopped and looked me in the eye and kind of gave a quick laugh and said, "Are you up to me wheeling the gurney into my office to show you something?"

I must have agreed because next thing I know is I was in his office, looking at a computer screen with a full color, moving picture of my heart beating on the screen. He then pointed up to the area near the top where I had seen the "Bling" moment and said this is fat. I said, "Oh my that is an awful lot of fat" He then said, "No, that is just the right amount of fat!"

He then pointed near the bottom and said, "This is also fat."

I then said again "Oh that is a lot of fat."

At that point he said again "No, that is also just the right amount of fat"

He went on to say "Look at it! It's beautiful! If I didn't know better, I would say God came in before me and did surgery and gave you a brand new heart!"

"No surgery?" I asked

"I think you've already had it," he said.

I don't remember much about the rest of the day except being amazed at what I had to comprehend.

God had come to the rescue.

Apparently He showed me the "Hand of God" come down and supernaturally perform a miracle and hand me a victory. A victory I had already thanked him for right in my living room during the attack. A victory that the devil meant to take me out.

My family had been called in. All the signs, enzymes , etc., said no to life and yet with God, ALL things are possible and God said yes to life!

Mark 5:34

34 And He said to her, "Daughter, your faith has made you well. Go in peace, and be healed of your affliction."

Another beautiful thing also happened.

A week later came a knock on my door. It was the young EMT that had worked so hard to save my life in the ambulance.

He asked if he could come in and I welcomed him in my home.

The young man went on to tell me something quite unexpected.

He said that after that ambulance ride, he told his wife, if that lady makes it, I will go to church with you. He said "You were so sure. You never wavered and I wanted some of that. I was sure you were gone. Not once but twice when your blood pressure dropped so very low."

Also to note was, that a day after the event, I was puzzled why the Lord had shown me the word Augurer in my spirit when they never augered out anything.

I then thought, "Wait, I do remember that I felt the Lord had misspelled the word? So I looked up the word using the perceived misspelling from the Lord.

Ha

Wonder of wonders. That word that I hung onto so much as a promise from the Lord meant something completely different when you used that spelling.

When spelled AUGURERER it was an ancient word for a priest or Holy person who was a prophet or foreteller of the Lord's things to come.

Huh…The Lords ways are higher than our ways for sure!

Isaiah 55:9

"For as the heavens are higher than the earth, so are My ways higher than your ways."

Key take away #24 The Lord knows how to spell. :)

Chapter 26 **The Soup Kitchen Dream**

Gary, my neighbor and future husband, and I had very common interests as we both had a lifelong interest in antiques, both being in the business for years.

We went to work together and started what would later become one the Midwest's largest wholesalers of architectural and unique antiques housed in 11 warehouses.

The way we would go to work each day back then was, we would meet at the truck at whatever time we had arranged the night before. It was easy as we were next door neighbors and shared a common driveway that forked and turned one way to his house on the East and mine on the West.

On this particular day we were to meet at eight. I was not late and neither was he.

"How was your evening?" he said entering the truck. "Gary, It was so much to comprehend.

I had a dream that was so real you could smell it, taste it, and touch it. I saw two specific buildings in Ottumwa,"

(40 minutes from our home.)

"We were inside and everything was all white. We were bustling, I tell you and people were eating and laughing. It was the cutest little restaurant. People were seated, eating, and we were serving them. What I remember most was EVERYBODY was happy!!!"

"So," he said jokingly "you think we are to start a restaurant?"

"No" I said "We are to start a soup kitchen. God wants us to start a soup kitchen and he even showed us what buildings"

Taken aback he said, "How do you even know the two buildings you saw are even available to use?"

"I don't" I said.

BIG SILENCE

"Sheri, why don't I just take you to Ottumwa right now and get this out of your system as those buildings are probably not even available…AND you know we do already have a job" he said nervously.

"Let's go" I said excited but also nervous.

On the way he spoke to me about how I had disliked very much working at the soup kitchen from a few years back when I had worked there.

I agreed that was true but somehow through the experience of this dream I feel the Lord has completely changed my heart AND the idea of what a soup kitchen should be like. It has to serve **love** with the food on the side.

Acceptance and love.

The rest of the ride was pretty quiet as we both were pondering what all this might mean for our life. I also believe Gary may have perhaps been counting on a bet within himself that this would all go away as soon as I figured out that the buildings were indeed not available and then life could go on as if nothing had been said.

Of course I am in part imagining what Garys thoughts were as I type this.

Meanwhile we arrived at Ottumwa and headed towards Main Street where the buildings in my dream sat side by side. We soon pulled onto Main Street and Gary parked before one of the buildings in my dream, which was a disaster, and we simultaneously saw a man in the window of the building next door, which was also the other building in my dream.

"Oh, someone is here" I said and Gary said "Run and see if he knows anything."

 I gained entrance to the second building and asked if the man in the window knew anything about the two buildings?

"Really?" he said

"I am just putting a for sale sign in this building"

"OHHHHHHHHHHHH WHAAAAAAAAT? REALLY?"

"Do you know anything about the building next door?" I said

"WELL, that is what this other for sale sign is for." He said and my JAW DROPPED!

Oh my goodness I thought. My heart was racing and then I asked to see the buildings.

He gave us a tour of both, told us about one building that has a renter and various things people talk about when they speak about real estate purchase.

By this time, this whole tornado of ideas had Garys attention. He knew this was of God and he was listening. We both were listening.

Then he told us the price and we left. Discouraged by the price we drove away.

We talked about the odds of two properties being sold by two different sellers and listed with the same agent. Also, us being the first to see either of them after being shown them both in a dream.

We were busy chattering, driving down Richmond Avenue and then I must have fallen asleep. Gary still talking, did not notice.

As quick as a I fell asleep. I had another dream. In this dream I was given a price to offer for both buildings.

As quickly as I went to sleep, I also awakened, Gary still talking and he had not even noticed that I had fallen asleep and was back awake with renewed energy on making a soup kitchen happen as obedience to the Lord.

I called the realtor who at the time was my friend and offered him the amount that had been told me in the dream.

He came unglued.

He told me it had not even been on the market for twelve hours and between the two properties, I was wanting the two parties that owned them to collectively drop the price $78,000.

"I'm not going to even write it up" he said, "I'm not going to waste their time."

"You have to." I said

He said, "How's that?"

"The law" I said

"I am making an offer and it is the law."

"I will call them and tell them this ridiculous offer," he said "but I will not waste my time, writing it up."

"Whatever." I replied, disheartened by the perceived attack.

Two days later he called me back on behalf of both sellers. Neither party had counter offered.

They both accepted.

THEY BOTH ACCEPTED!!!

Three weeks to the day of the dream, we closed on both properties. If you have ever closed on real estate and dealt with bringing abstracts up to date, you know that is really quick.

REALLY QUICK!!!

At closing, there was one more surprise.

It came with one more building in back that we did not realize was part of the property.

Gary upon looking at it proclaimed. "This is the soup kitchen, Sheri. This is why it looked so small on the inside, in your dream. It is small."

Psalm 37:4

Delight yourself in the Lord and he will give you the desires of your heart!

Ecclesiastes 5:3

For a dream comes with much business, and a fools voice with many words.

Daniel 1:7

As for these four youths, God gave them learning and skill in all literature and wisdom, and Daniel had understanding in all visions and dreams.

Key take away #25. Use wisdom and test your dreams to make sure they are biblical.

Chapter 26 Putting Together a Restaurant

Now the work began.Gary was on board and we had only $300 in our business account.

What do I do first? With so little money I really only had funds to destruct not construct.

I announced what we were going to do at Church (the church we pastor is in another county) and a man in the congregation who was not in the room during the announcement came up to me and said. Sheri I am in charge of a large group that needs to do community service, a lot of it. Is there anything we an do to help you?

I asked him if he liked our project and he had not even heard about it.

And so it started. God had sent him along with workers at just the right time. We agreed to start on Monday and that Monday, we all stood in a circle in the building that fronted main street, held hands and said a prayer.

A prayer of thanks,

A prayer of blessings,

A prayer of multiplication,

A prayer of provision.

Psalm 132:15

I will abundantly bless her provision; I will satisfy her poor with bread.

Key take away #26 Oh, how He blesses us with bread! (In more ways than one.)

Chapter 27 GOD Named it BLESSINGS

Blessings it was called, from day one & that is the name, without discussion that came from our mouth and Blessings it had.

One day Gary and I were at an architectural salvage store that sold old doors for $60-$90 each and as we were admiring them I saw a couple of the doors that were mounted and painted white, hanging on the wall. It gave me the idea that, that would look very cool if Blessings, our new venture was done in white, all white doors.

As I said this, the store manager who must have heard me said, "Would you like to panel in doors? "

"Yes," I said, "but as usual my appetite is bigger than my budget."

"Do it" she said, "For such a good project I will let you have any door in the store for $10 each."

Wow. They were marked, much, much more.

We left that day with around 40 doors, enough old trim to do the whole place and some porch trim and rail. We went crazy repurposing it. First thing we did was paint each door a beautiful fresh white.

One person helping said, "Wow, this is sure a lot of entrances," and I thought, "yes it is."

Revelation 3:20

Behold, I stand at the door and knock. If anyone hears My voice and opens the door, I will come in to him and dine with him, and he with Me.

Another thing said by the same girl who had come to volunteer from the halfway house. "I finally see why all the old repurposed house parts were used. When others discard things once broken and old, God knows they can be repurposed and made beautiful. That makes me comfortable here. I belong. I have purpose. I helped build this."

Key take away #27.   He wants to dine with you, to commune with you! He loves you! You have purpose!

Chapter 27 Only Ask HIM

In the dream about the soup kitchen I was told to ask of no one, except HIM. Easy enough I thought!

I had told Gary of this and then went on to tell him that this kitchen will only work if the larger churches sponsor us, as the other churches were not large enough to keep us going. In my mind no other way existed.

I was immediately to be tested on that theory.

A representative of one of those churches came in and said they wanted to help us out.

Great! I thought! They went on to say there was just one catch! They were going to have to be asked.

ASKED?

That was the one thing that I knew the Lord had asked me not to do in the dream. So I tried to be cagey and get around it.

"Well, I don't want to ask you" I said. "I would rather you give what you are comfortable with."

" NOPE!"

They weren't having it.

They said it again." We want to help you! In fact we want to be your biggest sponsor! BUT you have to ask."

"Really?" I thought

This was getting tricky. I had to have their support …I thought.

"Last chance" they said.

I tried another tact. "I would rather you give whatever God puts in your heart," I said.

Their response surprised me.

"Ask me now or I'm walking."

"I am sure it will take a lot to run this project but I am not comfortable asking for reasons of my own, " I said, "I appreciate you wanting to be our largest sponsor! I would just pray about it if I were you and then I don't have to ask!"

"You had your chance!" they said and abruptly turned and left.

Oh boy that did not go at all like I thought I needed it to.

Thus started my greatest lesson in FAITH! I had been obedient and only asked my father in heaven and now knew this project was not to rely on man!

But how? I was to find out!

I did however get a $10 check that day from a little , kind lady that was approaching her 90's named Francis Goode. We held up the check, thanked God for it and asked HIM to multiply it.

Boy, did He go to town on that request!

Luke 21:1 1And He looked up and saw the rich putting their gifts into the treasury, 2 and He saw also a certain poor widow putting in two mites. 3 So He said, "Truly I say to you that this poor widow has put in more than all; 4 for all these out of their abundance have put in offerings for God, but she out of her poverty put in all the livelihood that she had.

Key take away #28 God can multiply any or all given in LOVE. God multiplies in Love.

Eventually all that was given to start the kitchen was given without asking. So many were the beautiful hearts that give. Big Churches, little churches, individuals, businesses and groups, even the church I did not ask. I actually believe this was not about them as much as it was about my obedience. God can use any of us unwittingly.

Chapter 28 His Provision and Humor

It would be an understatement to say how the Lord backed this project. Everything started to fall into place. Equipment, labor, etc., we worked on it a little everyday for a year, each day before we went to work at our regular job.

One day, on our way to town (it is a 35 to 40 minute drive) we were talking and I said,"Gary, I don't know why we are even going in today. If we had to rub two nickels together to make a dime we could only come up with half of it. Why we don't even have enough money to buy a box of screws if we needed."

Gary, determined to not drop the ball for even a day replied "We can always have our workers paint bricks."

We rode the rest of the trip in silence pondering the enormity of what we had done....or gotten into.

We did indeed paint bricks individually on the outside of the building that day. All the workers lined up painting individual bricks.

Just then a van drove up and a man got out carrying a box ! I hollered "Hey Steve, whatcha got?"

He said, "Ooooh, something told me you might need a box of screws."

Ha!

Yes, God has a sense of humor!

Isaiah 46:10

Declaring the end from the beginning,

Key take away #29 God knows the end from the beginning and loves to give you pleasure. He can be funny too!

Chapter 29   POWER from GOD

The three buildings, it turns out are on the same electrical service and we did not have adequate electric for the three buildings combined if I was to run ovens, etc., as you would in a kitchen.

So the next thing to do was to find an electrician to change the service out to a larger one. We called an electrician and he left us a bid for $37,000.

Shocked, I called a second electrician. They met with us and let us know it would need to have a new larger line of service come in under the alley and the price was not going to be pretty. They would get back to us soon. They did get back to us and it was a nicely typed bid but the total still gave us an electric jolt at $42,000.

I let him out the door still reeling from the number on the page swirling in my head!

I said to Gary "What have I done" No quicker had that come from my mouth than my attention averted to a man running, or shuffle running rather, up the street towards the door that had not even had time to close behind the electrician who gave us the bid.

He came right up to the door and I said to him that I was sorry but we were not a business that was open and he said, "You need an electrician don't you?" I looked at Gary and he looked at me and we welcomed this man that I had never seen in our door.

He brought with him a flashlight and it turns out that he was agreeing with the other electricians assessment of our situation. It turns out he had been their teacher to become master electricians and proclaimed he did not teach any dummies. I asked him, while he was pointing a flashlight into a breaker box if he had any idea what it would cost to have him do this project.

At that point he stopped and turned to me and said

"Do you think I am going to charge the Lord who woke me up to come and do your electric?"

That meant it was on. All the labor was free and he paid for half the materials and we paid for the other half.

How is that for getting power! God's Power!

Psalm 62:11

Once God has spoken; twice have I heard this: that power belongs to God,

Exodus 14:14

The Lord will fight for you, and you have only to be silent.

Key take away #30   A better life I could not live than the life of walking with the Lord knowing that All things are possible to those who believe.

Chapter 30 Hot and Cold

The interior was coming right along. We paneled with the doors, made a bar to eat at out of doors, and made our double oven cabinet out of doors. By putting in a handicap accessible bathroom we had only a small space above the bathroom for a furnace.

I got a call from a man who had been in the VA hospital in Iowa City two hours away and the Lord had put it on his heart to give this random project a furnace and central air without even being asked.

We placed it in what amounted to the size of a crawl space above the bathroom and we placed a porch railing, painted the matching white in front of it to camouflage it yet allow for the air to freely flow in this space that was quite frankly turning into a cute little bistro.

In fact, if it had been located in France you would have written home to say you ate in the cutest little bistro that was made of all repurposed house parts.

The project, which was dedicated to the Lord, was turning into a project you would be pleased to present to the Lord.

Colossions 3:23 And whatever you do, do it heartily, as to the Lord and not to men, Do as if unto the Lord.

Key take away #30 If you do whatever you do as if unto the Lord, you will find yourself wasting a lot less time as you will choose all you do much more wisely.

Chapter 31   Supernatural provision

We opened with only $77 dollars in our budget to run the place, but we decided to go ahead as God had built our faith up pretty big by now and I was learning that I really could rely on him.

We gave five promotional dinners by invitation for pastors, city officials, and grocers to let them know and experience what we were up to. The numbers started small running around 20 people and grew to numbers which averaged between 150-300 people a day. We wore uniform shirts, poured their drinks, made and served home made butter daily, waited on their tables and ran it like any restaurant complete with pie or dessert.

I wanted people treated as you would be treated in the nicest of restaurants. Even with those wild swings in numbers, never once did we run out of food.

NOT ONCE!!

Hundreds and hundreds of times though we served the last spoon to the last person.

Mathew 14 13-20

13 When Jesus heard *it,* He departed from there by boat to a deserted place by Himself. But when the multitudes heard it, they followed Him on foot from the cities. 14 And when Jesus went out He saw a great multitude; and He was moved with compassion for them, and healed their sick. 15 When it was evening, His disciples came to Him, saying, "This is a deserted place, and the hour is already late. Send the multitudes away, that they may go into the villages and buy themselves food."

16 But Jesus said to them, "They do not need to go away. You give them something to eat."

17 And they said to Him, "We have here only five loaves and two fish."

18 He said, "Bring them here to Me." 19 Then He commanded the multitudes to sit down on the grass. And He took the five loaves and the two fish, and

looking up to heaven, He blessed and broke and gave the loaves to the disciples; and the disciples gave to the multitudes. 20 So they all ate and were filled, and they took up twelve baskets full of the fragments that remained. 21 Now those who had eaten were about five thousand men, besides women and children.

Key take away #30 God WANTS you to learn to multiply to advance the kingdom.

One time God told me to "learn to multiply". I heard this in my spirit and my life has never been the same since.

Chapter 33   God's Multiplication

One day a sweet gal I worked with, named Mary Ann, asked me after a particularly busy feeding frenzy day of serving up beef and noodles how we paid for all of this.

We had cooked, plated up, and served over 300 people. On this particular day Mary Ann turned to me and said . "We served a lot of food. How do you pay for all of this? Who sponsors this?"

I then pointed to the sky.

She said , "I know, but who REALLY sponsors this?"

Well, Mary Ann, it costs between around $300 a day to run this place. At that point I reached in my pocket to show my receipt of how much I had in the bank on that day for Blessings. I had run through the bank drive up and had asked my balance.

The receipt read $14.99.

"You're CLOSING?" She exclaimed.

"NO" I told her. I am showing you, so you will believe me on who sponsors this.

"Well, how will you cover tomorrow?" She said

"Thats what I have learned to do" I said, "I have learned to know it will always be covered. I have learned to have FAITH! All I know is by morning, I will have enough money to run the kitchen." We then parted for the day, her to a two week vacation of a mission in South Dakota and me to Sonic Happy hour for a half priced Raspberry tea.

Parting Mary Ann said, "You have to let me know how this turns out."

I know it was not 2 o'clock yet because I was still awaiting happy hour for my tea. Happy hour starts at 2 and I was still sitting in the Walgreen parking lot waiting when my phone rang.

"Sheri?"

"Yes" I said

"This is Tom, manager at (a local corporation). You have won the grant!"

I said, "GREAT, but I didn't apply for a grant."

He said,
"Thats a problem" he went onto explain that I needed to go online and fill out the grant application.

I assured him that I would try to have it filled by the following Friday.

"No" he said "The Lord wants me to give you $1500 by 8:30 in the morning."

I could not wait until I could tell Mary Ann the rest of the story. God really knows how to multiply.

Matthew 14:13-21 Feeding the Five Thousand

When Jesus heard *it,* He departed from there by boat to a deserted place by Himself. But when the multitudes heard it, they followed Him on foot from the cities. And when Jesus went out He saw a great multitude; and He was moved with compassion for them, and healed their sick. When it was evening, His disciples came to Him, saying, "This is a deserted place, and the hour is already late. Send the multitudes away, that they may go into the villages and buy themselves food." 16 Jesus replied, "They do not need to go away. You give them something to eat."

17 "We have here only five loaves of bread and two fish," they answered.

18 "Bring them here to me," he said. **19** And he directed the people to sit down on the grass. Taking the five loaves and the two fish and looking up to heaven, he gave thanks and broke the loaves. Then he gave them to the disciples, and the disciples gave them to the people. **20** They all ate and were satisfied, and the disciples picked up twelve basketfuls of broken pieces that were left over. **21** The number of those who ate was about five thousand men, besides women and children.

Key: All good things can be multiplied, when held up to the Lord, blessed, given thanks for and asked to be multiplied.

Chapter 34   The vacationers

One day at the soup kitchen a nicely dressed couple came in and I complemented the lady's cute outfit. I sat a meal before each of them and asked what they may like for dessert. They looked up at each other seemingly a bit surprised and then they commenced eating.

When they were nearing completion of their meal I asked if they would like seconds?

They declined. "Egg salad?" I said, "Delicious."

Then the man took me up on the egg salad sandwich.

"Is this your first time here?" I asked

Then the story came out. By then volunteers Heidi Altfillisch and Leisa Walker had tuned in to hear.

The couple was from Ames and had left for vacation that very morning. They checked the internet for good restaurants when they got near Ottumwa and were getting hungry. They saw Blessings Soup Kitchen was

4.9 stars and decided to go there. They were embarrassed to say they did not realize it was an actual soup kitchen as it was so cute. Well, we all had a fun laugh and I gave them a tour and took them to the coffee shop.

They said they now already had a good vacation story.

Blessings Soup Kitchen is for everyone!

God is good!

Acts 10:34
Then Peter opened his mouth, and said, Of a truth I perceive that God is no respecter of persons.

Romans 9:38
For I am persuaded, that neither death, nor life, nor angels, nor principalities, nor powers, nor things present, nor things to come,
39 Nor height, nor depth, nor any other creature, shall be able to separate us from the love of God, which is in Christ Jesus our Lord.

Key take away #33 God loves you whether you are poor or well off. He loves YOU rich or poor. He wants you fed. He wants you loved!

Chapter 35   Moravian Falls

Lying in bed one night I was awake and became aware of a very strong presence. I heard what seemed a female voice speak to me very directly. She said three things.

1. "Go to Moravian Falls"

2. "Pitch a tent"

3. "Build a church"

As she (female sounding voice) spoke I literally shook. REALLY, REALLY SHOOK! It was so intense I turned away from the voice and kept my face to the mattress and continued to shake. I saw no one. At its finish I immediately got up and wrote the above things down.

I did not know what any of it meant. I had heard of a school nearby called Moravia but was lost as to why it would have been called Moravian Falls. Confused I got up the next morning and looked up the term Moravian Falls.

Upon looking up the term I found that it is a small town located in North Carolina at the foothills of the Brushy Mountain range in the Appalachian Mountains. When looked up on the internet I found it to be a small burg, nestled in the foothills with history rich in prayer. The Moravians had settled there and bought hundreds if not thousands of acres and prayed 24/7 for over 150 years. They were said to have created an open heaven with more angel sitings to the area than anywhere else in the U. S. This was October of 2011.

I was pondering all of this and kept mulling this over in my mind to figure out what to do and how to make all this work. I wanted to be obedient but how do I just take off from work and go somewhere I do not know and pitch a tent, let alone build a church. If I were to leave immediately saying a little voice told me I thought I may be locked up with the key thrown away. I did not want to be the crazy lady. I told no one except my business and co pastor Gary Smith, who listened intently with very little response. I found that comforting in that he did not have me hauled away. He merely listened.

Pretty soon time had grown close to Thanksgiving and I got caught up in the preparations you would for family gatherings that occur at the holidays. Thanksgiving gave way to Christmas and pretty soon it was January and I had done nothing relevant to the incident.

The only other person I confided the story to my daughter who said "Mom, if God is sending you on a field trip I want to go too." That made me very happy!

That was a better response than I had expected and so I started to make plans to go and see what it was about. We decided on a particular weekend in March, and so I called to make reservations to stay at wherever I could find in this small town. I found the name of a place and called them. It so happened they were located right by the water fall the town was named after. The lady doing the reservations said all their weekends were booked up well in advance so I would not be able to stay the weekend we had decided.

"Wait a minute" she said, "Let me check for sure. What date did you say? Thats odd," she said in her strong southern accent, "that date is erased and open. Well, I guess you can have it if you want." And so it was that on that weekend in May we set out on our journey.

We got plane tickets to go to Moravian Falls North Carolina, a town I had never heard of until the voice the previous fall spoke. Excited about the trip we set out to pack. Prior to the flight I had three visions.

The first vision was one of a giant wheel.

The second was an impression of my daughters face coming out of a body of water.

The third was a white car that said Moravian Falls on the side and it was pulling a trailer of sticks.

I did not know what to make of any of them.

YET...I was soon to find out.

I also was given the scripture

2 Chronicles 1-4 and it read

1 And Solomon the son of David was strengthened in his kingdom, and the Lord his God was with him, and magnified him exceedingly.

2 Then Solomon spake unto all Israel, to the captains of thousands and of hundreds, and to the judges, and to every governor in all Israel, the chief of the fathers.

3 So Solomon, and all the congregation with him, went to the high place that was at Gibeon; for there was the tabernacle of the congregation of God, which Moses the servant of the Lord had made in the wilderness.

4 But the ark of God had David brought up from Kirjathjearim to the place which David had prepared for it: for he had pitched a tent for it at Jerusalem.

The scripture I was given was also where David had pitched a tent…interesting.

The plane ride was exciting as my daughter and I did not know what to expect. I told her about the vision I had of her face coming out of water and said I did not want to talk her in to anything but told her I believed it meant I was to baptize her. She grinned and that was all there was to that conversation. I was not sure where my daughter stood on many issues. I had hardly had time to sort my own.

We got to the airport, rented a car and immediately drove to Moravian Falls. It was evening and by the time we got to our destination it was after midnight. We drove up to the place and could immediately hear the sound of rushing water from the falls. We were shown our cabin and to our delight it was just a few steps from the falls.

Our cabin was beautifully appointed with no detail left undone.

One thing was strange though. The atmosphere was thick with what I would call tangible glory when we got there. Immediately I was absorbed into the atmosphere. Lifting my hands to him I was sharply startled out of the moment by my daughter who exclaimed she thought she was dizzy or ill from the elevation or mountain drive. She decided to step outside to catch her balance and take in different air. She stepped outside and immediately came back inside. She said, "Mom, it is not the same out there as it is in here. Is this what you feel when you say you feel God's presence?"

Indeed she had nailed it right on the head. All of a sudden the words God had given us before our flight there seemed to come to life in that

Ark of the covenant where David had prepared where they had **pitched a tent?**

Happy, we decided to go to bed and awaken Saturday morning to see what it all was about. I laid my head on my pillow and before I could go to sleep I heard a plethora of voices of many tenors and tones saying hi, how are you and many other greetings. The sound was so happy and friendly that I started off to sleep.

Once again before sleep was imminent I saw a spiraling whirlwind of white and gold tunneling up to the sky like a vortex..the ceiling seemed gone during this action and then it was back to normal. Exhausted and happy I went immediately to sleep by Sally.

The next morning we awakened to the sound of the falls once again. We enjoyed some food and proceeded out to explore the world. The falls were beautiful and we were staying just a few yards from it. By the falls was a water wheel which was just like the wheel I had seen in my spirit and I knew we were at the right place.

We walked around, looking and enjoying the falls and Sally said she would like to be baptized. We then pitched a small tent for obedience sake near the falls that we had purchased at a local Walmart on the way up the mountain. We lay lazily in the tent, reading the word, intermittently getting out to explore the beautiful area.

Upon inspection Sally decided the water was pretty cold as it had come down from the mountain. I said it may be too cold for you to be baptized and she said no Mom you just sprinkle water on my forehead, I saw it done at my friend's church.

I said no that is not how the bible says to baptize and we tossed ideas a bit back and forth about it. I said Sally, you just call Pastor Gary to see what he says. Upon reaching her dear Gary he confirmed that the Bible says to do a full immersion.

She accepted that but wondered why and then became concerned about the waters temperature.

She decided she would do it BUT we would have to wait until four o clock when she perceived that the water would be its warmest and we would have to be very quick about it so it would not to be dangerous. At the conclusion of this discussion we went back to our cabin. Happily we sat down to enjoy our cozy cabin and Sally grabbed a bible to as she put it" just see if God has anything He wants to say to us". She closed her eyes and started to thumb through the pages. Still with eyes closed she turned page after page, took her finger and pointed, opened her eyes and read right out of Romans where it spoke of baptism.

"Mom,`God really spoke to us."

 We then became quite fired up for the baptism and I walked to the office to make sure that it was ok to get in the water.

Anita and Ken were the owners of the park and Anita explained to me that it was against the rules to baptize there for liability sake . I said I understood and she said, "Why did I want to baptize there?"

I told her and she said, "Well that is different if God sent you."

"Go right ahead. You tell God that's just fine." That made me chuckle, she was so sweet.

We continued to explore, collect rocks and read from the Bible. As the day passed tourists came and went and soon it was to be four o'clock, the hour Sally had chosen to be baptized.

We dressed in shorts and grabbed our towels and started toward the basin at the bottom of the falls. Two people were still there as we approached. They were sitting at a picnic table talking while a man walked around taking pictures. I was rather embarrassed and did not want to get into the water while they were there so I proposed waiting a few feet from them behind a bush until they left.

Waiting patiently they seemed to not be ready to leave and Sally, frustrated said that at 4 o'clock the water would start turning the other way on temperature.

Convinced she was right, I decided to approach the two ladies at the table to tell them what our plans were and they would perhaps leave.

Upon arrival at the table I learned one lady's name was Dana and she was from Lincolnton, North Carolina, a two hour drive away and the other was from Wisconsin with her picture taking husband.

What they said next would change the course of history in my world and Sally's.

They each said they had not previously known each other but while driving their individual vehicles they heard a female sounding voice tell them to go to Moravian Falls to witness a 4 o'clock baptism.

"My Goodness, repeat that? Thats what I thought you said." I went to get Sally.

I introduced them to Sally and asked them to repeat what they said again to her. In joy we all went down to the banks of the creek. They were just as happy and excited about the mystery revealing itself as we were. We prayed, went in the water and took pictures. This was a real event and Dana has come back and attended a few of my evangelism events, and is part of one of my testimonies, but that is getting ahead of myself. Needless to say it was a wonderful trip.

Sally was baptized and we flew back in time that I was still able to preach in my home church on Sunday evening. Sally asked if she could read the Romans scripture to the congregation as it was so important to her and now important to share.

Now when we go back and evangelize our Dana from Lincolnton, NC, the baptism witness, comes along to confirm!

As for the visions I had seen, well, the wheel was right by the falls where it had been powered for years by the water coming down the mountain.

The white suburban I had seen pulling a trailer of sticks was there and gathering sticks by Ken the owner when I arrived.

The baptism of my daughter that I saw coming out of the water actually happened. God actually sent witnesses to confirm everything from different locations at just the right time.

The bank of Angels that greeted me was amazing and the Lord met us with all his glory when we arrived as in the scripture where David pitched a tent.

It was an awesome field trip for the Lord.

Key take away #35 The Holy Spirit is with you every step of the way! Obedience is big!

Chapter 36   Jesus's Face

I like dogs. I really do. I have a basset hound named Jack and then I got a beagle named Jimmy as his friend. They got along famously until the neighbor's dog Thor and Jimmy took off for a day that turned into several. Although I was actively trying to find him, I seemed to be always just behind him. Going door to door asking and flyering, had anyone seen my pup? I had a vision that night of my pup on my lap in the car but I told Gary my take on seeing this vision was that I was pulling back from a pup that I should have been happy to find and wondered what that meant. Why would I not want my pup?

The next night a lady called who had seen my flyer posted at the local beauty salon and thought she had my dog! Upon arrival I found a dog that was without collar and very similar in markings to mine. I said it was not mine and she told me he was a stray that she could no longer keep. She said she had begged her husband to let her catch him and call me as she had seen his picture posted at the hair salon. I told her he was not mine and she begged me to take the pup with me so that her husband would not stay mad at her. I decided to take him and flyer on his behalf as well so that all persons involved including this similar to my pup could also find his home. Now I understood my vision.

I did not find my dog. The newly acquired little homeless dog had no one call for him either so I kept him.

He immediately became fast friends with Jack (my other dog) and they played together every day. He was a funny little dog but somehow I became VERY attached. He seemed so excited about every little bit of attention.

One day we had clients in from Texas and Johnny (the pup's new name) kept getting out of the fenced in yard and playing with my clients. They were making over him and I was making over him. He was also scoring very well on the summer sausage snacks that we get at the local meat market to host our clients (antique dealers). As dog days goes, Johnny pup was doing all the fun stuff. He was running rabbits, streaking, jumping in out of arms and quite frankly having the best day a dog could have. My little orphan was having a blast. At the end of the day, my clients trailer was all loaded, (We are antique wholesalers) Johnny was still jumping in and out of our arms and streaking with delight. We all decided to go to supper together and Johnny got put back with Jack in the yard and all was great.

During our meal, Gary received a call and Johnny had escaped, ran in front of a car on the highway, and was killed immediately.

The girl on the phone said that Jack, the basset that was still alive, was moaning uncontrollably as he saw it happen. I hurried home and went sobbing to the Lord.

Why? Why? Why? Then I cried and cried and cried. That night I was lying in bed and still crying and beside me I saw the face of the Lord as if lying beside me on my pillow, with TEARS coming down his cheeks. I went to sleep comforted in HIS presence.

Revelation 7:17

For the Lamb at the center of the throne will be their shepherd; he will lead them to the springs of Living Water , and God will wipe away every tear!

Psalm 56:8
You number my wanderings; Put my tears into Your bottle; Are they not in Your book

He loves us so much!

Key take away #36 He sure does love us and our tears matter!

Chapter 37 **The Healing Part One**

My clients were upset about Johnny also and had bonded throughout the day. That said it was time for them to go on from there as they were headed on to Minnesota to see Rex's parents. Rex (not his real name) had been having a sore throat recently and was to possibly have his tonsils removed upon getting back to Texas. He was wearing a scarf around his neck to keep it warm. He said it was because it was so cold here (mid November in Iowa vs Texas) and they were coming from a hot climate. We parted company that night in tears because of Johnny's death and all agreed that as days go, Johnny's (the pup's) last day must have been such a happy one.

A couple of weeks went by and the phone rang. I saw it was Rex and answered in kind of a silly way. Immediately I knew it was not a silly kind of phone call.

Rex related to me that he had just been diagnosed with stage four esophageal cancer. He had called to ask if I would pray for him. I was so shook up by his call that I told him I needed to compose myself a bit to pray and would call him back shortly.

Wow, I thought to myself. He is such a strong and viral man. Standing 6'4" tall, approximately 290 lbs., he was ALL man. He just kept saying I am not sure how to pray but I know you do and I need you to tell HIM, I believe, I believe, I believe.

At that point he was in tears, I was trying to not show that I was in tears. He kept saying all the things he had left to do. I got off the phone in disbelief and went across the property to find Gary, to tell him the news and get him in on the prayer.

Gary is a man of God, with big faith and is also a prayer warrior. We called Rex back together and prayed with him. Rex had completely dissolved to tears by this time. By the time I got off of the phone I was emotionally wiped out and retreated to have a talk with God of my own. I realized this was one of the most serious things I had ever been asked to pray for.

My mother Shirley had just passed away from esophageal cancer and this brought back a flood of emotions and memories. I had prayed for healings before. Some with results and some not. I was sure that God wants His people well so any poor results may have been from some lacking on my part. The bible promises healing but what can stop it. I remember that those things that are the largest mountains in our life go with both prayer and fasting. With full resolve, I decided to give fasting with prayer a try!

That Sunday I asked for a silent prayer for a healing as a congregation and spoke with God myself (not that I did anything for this) and promised Him a 40 Day fast for consideration of a healing. This Cancer seemed like as big a mountain as one could ask for. Stage 4 throat cancer is not good. Rex had explained they were not even going to do treatment but he did ask them to and paid cash for the procedure. His insurance had a $2000 limit for cancer. Well, that was my prayer and a few other things were also included.

Life went on and, well if you have ever fasted for something with God you know that the longer you give up something of the flesh the closer you get with God.

I was having increased visions and specific revelations about my own health. These things that I was being shown about myself I took so serious as to check them out with my doctor only to find out they were true before I even showed any symptoms.

Well, anyway, one night I had a very vivid vision while awake. I was in what I thought was my own throat looking all around. Sounds strange, I know, it was.

It seems I was standing at the very back of my tongue and saw clutter being swept away. Clutter like red bumps, black spots, white places (bacteria I thought). Sweeping,

sweeping,

sweeping.

I could hear it and then I saw the letters **tx** appear at the top of the throat. Then the vision was over and the next morning as I got on the truck to work with Gary, I exclaimed that I had a vision.

I proclaimed that God loves me so much that he had shown me that I had bacteria on the back of my tongue. He must be telling me I have bad breath and showed me how to brush way back. I told Gary I had tried it but when I brushed that far back I had literally gagged. I said it was going to be hard to do.

I am not sure when, I had the OMG moment.

It is embarrassing to say that I had to go this far at all. I tell you the previous to let you know that this experience was so foreign to me that I called it wrong. Anyway, when I got it I finally exclaimed out loud in the truck.

"Rex is HEALED!"

The Lord showed me he cleaned out Rex's throat. I am such a dummy I thought he was showing me something about myself.

I was beside myself with this. I called my daughter who had recently started realizing that the Lord was giving me information that could not be that accurate on my own. When I told her, we were so happy. I said I cannot believe I did not realize it immediately because the Lord even wrote Tx so that I would receive this vision about Rex as he is from Texas.

She said, "Mom, Tx is shorthand in the medical field for treatment, I use that terminology all the time in my patient notes."

Wow, either way, Texas or treatment or both I was ecstatic. That Sunday in church it was day 40 of my fast and I announced with much enthusiasm that I had been shown Rex's healing. My daughter asked me when I was going to tell Rex and I said I was not. I would wait to hear from him.

That was January and it was two more months before I would hear from Rex. In fact so much time had passed that I now felt it was awkward for me to ask how he was doing after so long.

Gary and I are probably the Midwest's largest wholesalers of unique, antique things and make our living by trucks pulling in trailers and filling them with merchandise for show or their stores. The month of March is particularly busy as there are some very big shows that happen throughout the nation including Warrenton, Texas. I was excited for what I knew to be true, but I was not prepared for what was to come next.

Psalm 30:2

O Lord my God, I cried out to You and you Healed me.

Psalm 9:10

And those who know Your name will put their trust in You; For You, Lord have not forsaken those who seek You.

Key take away #37   His love is so GREAT and He will not forsake you!

Chapter 38   The Healing Part two

On March 24, my birthday, I had a very clear vision of myself on a church pew with hands raised. As I was praising God without any part of my body moving, (I was in a seated position with my hands raised) I started sliding , in that seated position, with hands up from the left side of the pew, slowly down to the right.

 Upon reaching the right end of the pew, I slowly started moving left until I had slid (with arms extended upward) to the starting place at the left end of the pew or beginning position. When I reached my original position in the vision I looked at where I had been and saw a spot on the pew at the other end.

The people in the pew behind with arms still raised were exclaiming. I see evidence. This is evidence. That brought to mind a scripture.

Hebrews 11:1

Now faith is the substance of things hoped for, the evidence of things not seen.

I got up to look this up in scripture, excited because God had just given me a mystery. I was looking it up on the internet at approximately 3AM. As I was reading the scripture my instant messenger bell went off and I checked my email.

It was Rex. He was at the Texas show in Warrenton and had lost 70 lbs, was very weak and had a feeding tube, BUT he had news that outside his family he wanted me to hear. He had just had a test to see where all the cancer had spread and to determine how long he had left to live.

"Sheri," he said, "you are the only one who will believe this because you and Gary were the only ones who said this could happen. Not only had it not spread it is not there at all. No trace. No trace of cancer at all. I still have the feeding tube but please tell God. I am so happy. I want to thank you so much."

I told Rex, It was not me and we had so much to tell him when we next saw him.

I did not tell him at that time about the vision or the fast. I was not sure what to do at that point. Not everyone is into miracles, signs and wonders.

Then I thought of the beautiful vision God gave me about faith being the substance of things hoped for and the evidence of things not seen. At that moment I realized that God had just shown me we do not have to be at the place to see a prayer answered. Gary and I praying and fasting in Iowa, to God in heaven can heal in Texas.

Marvelous.

Matthew 17:20
So Jesus said to them, "Because of your unbelief; for assuredly, I say to you, if you have faith as a mustard seed, you will say to this mountain, 'Move from here to there,' and it will move; and nothing will be impossible for you."

Matthew 17:21"However, this kind does not go out except by prayer and fasting."

Key take away # 38   How magnificent is the Lord!

Chapter 39 **The rest of the story**

In June they came back. Rex had lost even more weight and was now down 90 lbs, but I was so happy to see him. I asked Gary if I could tell Rex this testimony of events. It seemed to me the whole purpose for the healing was not just for him to be healed but for others to be strengthened in their belief.

Gary said this is kind of touchy to mix business with this kind of thing so he asked me to hold on and play it by ear. Usually I am very much into sales but on this day I just kept watching Rex and his wife.

So happy, so full of life and I just wanted them to know that God is real, that this is truly a miracle not a coincidence. After going through the first warehouse (we had nine at the time) and on our way to the next, by trucks, I said, "Gary, may I tell them yet?"

Gary being all business at that moment thought it would derail the whole sale. So I prayed. I need an opening God. They are all about buying product today.

We are all about selling and this is so hard. An opening wasn't naturally happening.

This, unlike today, had never been my forte. To pick up and turn the subject to God, to people that I don't know whether or not they believe in this manner.

At the second warehouse I kept looking at Gary as if to ask now? May I now? Gary was getting exasperated with me I could tell. I completely lost nerve at that point and went to sit down. I chose a seat on a shoe shine pedestal chair, where I could see the whole warehouse number 2 and write down their purchases while they were making them. I was becoming resigned that this was neither the time nor the place but still having an ongoing internal dialog with myself and God on what to do.

"Lord this is a beautiful testimony but if this will turn these people off I understand".

Then I went back to my job.

Rex's wife was very busy color coordinating and putting a mental picture of her booth items together and trying to coordinate it as she purchased. Right at the moment she was standing in an all black furniture item section, with one cream and green piece for coffee display to her right which she really seemed to like.

"Ok, God." I said, "I am not going to do this unless you want me to. I will not say anything to them unless Rex's wife Lilly says the word **Red**". A color that was only seen in that building on a couple of item's.

"Ok Sheri, back to work." I said to myself.

"Lilly did you decide on that coffee piece?" I asked. It was 4 foot by 3 feet, green and cream and she was standing right in front of it.

Lilly replied " The **RED** one?"

I about fell out of my chair " The **RED** one?" I repeated "do we have a **red** one?"

She said, "Yes, clear back at the back."

Now this was a very small piece and I had not even seen it for months because of size and placement, underneath some other items.

"Ok!" I said, interrupting everyone .

That was clearly my sign to proceed . All their chit chat ceased as I spoke (Gary was into his chit chat) but with as much authority as I could place in my voice. I said "I have to change the subject"

"Oh No" I could see it in Gary's face but there was no turning back now without looking like an idiot. Gary about swallowed his teeth. There was no stopping once I started. The place went quiet and **everyone**, Rex, Lilly and Gary just looked at me as if to say what is more important than what we are doing.

They had driven hours here and this is what they were here to do. Seriously you could have heard a pin drop and I could not look at Gary because I had to proceed whether he was in or not. Gulp!

I told Rex and Lilly I needed to tell him something that I was kind of afraid to tell them. I said, "Do you remember when you called last November and asked me to pray?" He said, 'yes" and the silence at this point was louder than any noise I had ever heard.

 I told him about the fast and the vision and about the sweeping in the throat. Now this is a very fine line to walk between faith and getting committed for being crazy if people do not believe in visions. I just went there with one of our largest clients. Rex immediately tuned in and was so focused I felt we were locked together as I told my side of his story. He started weeping and gave me the biggest hug. I told him God loved him so much that when he prayed he wanted him healed and wanted others to know who did it.

By then I had the courage to look around and saw that Gary, Lilly AND Rex were all crying. It was a beautiful cry though and God's presence was very evident. We ended in a very good spiritual place and hugs were exchanged by all.

The peace that came over that building in that moment could have been cut and served on a platter. It was marvelous and we ALL felt it.

Here is the part that has really stuck with me. Sobbing he walked over to me and asked why I had not told him sooner or right away.

I said, "I guess I only had enough faith for me." Rex repeated what I said and kind of laughed. He said that seemed so honest. He said it would have had to be huge faith to carry all of them. That is the beautiful part though. I told him " I now have HUGE faith because of this and now know I can, with God's help slay any dragon that comes my way or anyone else's."

God is so good.

Matthew 15:28

Then Jesus answered and said to her, "O woman, great is your faith! Let it be to you as you desire." And her daughter was healed from that very hour.

Key take away #37 : HE IS SO GREAT! Have faith for there is nothing He cant do! He will also guide your words so that you may say just the right thing!

Chapter 38   The Song

Doing what I do at the soup kitchen is difficult sometimes and sometimes you deal with ALL sorts of mental or emotional or substance abuse issues.

One time, I was attacked physically by someone unexpectedly and at that particular moment there was nothing to do but defend myself. As I recall it ended with us physically wrestling on the floor. I was so upset and traumatized when it was over that I just cried and cried.

Then I heard this song in my spirit…

"Get yourself up ((bum bum bum) percussive sounds) Dust yourself off ((Bum Bum Bum) more percussive sounds) and Start All over again!

What else could I do? I got up and started all over again.

2 Corinthians 12:9

9 But he said to me, "My grace is sufficient for you, for my power is made perfect in weakness." Therefor I will boast all the more gladly about my weaknesses, so that Christ's power may rest on me.

Key take away #38

He can renew you and give you the strength to go on!

Chapter 41 Spiritual Warfare

Tonight I lie in wait as last night I saw a tornado, before me in my spirit. Last time that happened I became in the middle of huge spiritual warfare. In my spirit I had seen our church completely decimated by whirling wind with one lady left in the middle.

I perceived that she was the reason for the storm. I was told that she had a Chaldean spirit and to guard the gates. I had many things happen that week that were not for the faint of heart but on Thursday evening of that week while in prayer I heard the words "it is broken"and saw a broom fall from the sky in my spirit and fall to the floor. Shortly after, she left the church and all returned to normal. We were later to find she was claiming demons and witchcraft.

2 Timothy 3:16

All scripture is God breathed and is useful for teaching, rebuking, correcting and training in righteousness.

Ephesians 6:12

For we do not wrestle against flesh and blood, but against principalities, against powers, against the rulers of the darkness of this age, against spiritual hosts of wickedness in the heavenly places.

Ephesians 6:13-15

13 Therefore take up the whole armor of God, that you may be able to withstand in the evil day, and having done all, to stand.
14 Stand therefore, having girded your waist with truth, having put on the breastplate of righteousness,
15 and having shod your feet with the preparation of the gospel of peace

Key take away #41   God will let you know through the Holy Spirit how to discern between light and dark. The word lets us know how to protect ourselves. Put on the whole armor of God.

Chapter 42 The Vision of a Book

The Big Miracle Part One

I had a vision and in the vision, I saw the front of a book. It had a table of contents on the front that said Angels, Visions and Dreams around and along a road. I saw this and I was told in my spirit to write and go to Moravian falls, North Carolina again.

I also saw the name **Caroline Peacher** written in my spirit. This was on a Friday night and I immediately got out of bed where the spirit lead me to write 24 pages of experience by experience , testimonies with the contents of the title as the theme. I had no idea why I was to go back to Moravian Falls, North Carolina, I felt it was about this book the Lord wanted me to write but really...why go to Moravian Falls to write it?

By Sunday I had written 42 pages on the subjects suggested by the Holy Spirit. I thought I would look at the area and see if there were any events that fit my schedule. I typed in Moravian Falls and low and behold, there was a Christian Writers convention by one of my favorite prophets holding a convention that week in Moravian Falls. The convention was being held by Rick Joyner of Morning Star Ministries of Charlotte North Carolina.

The conference was $1000 and I had $300 in my checking account. That settled it. I did not have enough money for airfare at that late date let alone the $1,000 necessary for the conference fee.

Still I kept thinking about it and by Monday morning I had checked out airfare costs. Without the usual two weeks notice the lowest cost I could find was still over $500. Ok, I thought, I really cannot go even if the Lord suggested it.

It was Monday morning, the conference was Thursday, I did not have but $300. It was 9:00 AM and I needed to go to work, as we had a client coming in a few minutes for a day of purchasing antiques wholesale from us to sell retail in their store. It would be a big day of shopping by them, loading their trailer, and having fun in general because that's what we do. My business partner/co-pastor set out for the warehouses to meet our client for a day of sales. Everything was going very well that day and I thoroughly enjoyed being with our clients Jo Jo and Kasey as always.

Still, I was distracted thinking about how it would have been such a great thing to do as God had suggested, had I been able to afford it! Waiting at one warehouse for my client to catch up with us at that location, I began to pray.

"Lord if I am to do this it would have to be all from You as I have no way to pull this off. I love You."

My client showed up and it was back to business . Loading, shopping, loading, shopping. By now it was 3:30 PM on Monday afternoon before I was able to think about the trip suggestion by the Lord again.

The conference was to start Thursday Morning in Moravian Falls. By 4 o clock we were done with sales and loading out of the last warehouse when I told Jo Jo that I would like to make a call before a business closed if she did not mind. She said it was no problem and I went to my car to see if I could at least find out a few things.

I decided to call Morningstar Ministries to see if there were even any openings left available for the conference. Their website said they were only accepting 20 people for the event.

I called information and asked for Morningstar Ministries main office number in Charlotte, North Carolina. The operator said she did not have anything under that heading(I had actually called information for the wrong town. Their ministry headquarters are located in Fort Mill , South Carolina which makes the rest of this story even more of a miracle.)

The operator said, "Would you like to be connected with Morning Light storage facility?"

I said, "No, I need MorningSTAR Ministries".

She said, "One moment please."

I waited on the line and it began to ring. A woman answered as if from a residential number.

"Hello?" she said

I said, "Oh, I must have been given a wrong number and began to apologize.

She said, "Who are you trying to reach?"

I said, "I was trying to reach Morning Star ministries in Charlotte NC."

It was momentarily quiet when she interrupted the silence with "How did you get this number?"

I explained "I was given a wrong number and connected by the operator. "

BIG SILENCE

She said, "That is a huge coincidence as I work for that ministry but I am two hours away in Moravian Falls at our lodge opening it up to air it out for a few minutes, to get it ready for a conference Thursday. Why are you trying to reach them?" she said

I said, "I was trying to see about getting in the writers conference and did not know if it was still possible."

"Oh my," she said, "I am in charge of that."

"I will give you a number to call . They think it is sold out but I have another bed available if you do not mind sleeping in a twin. The number is xxx xxx xxxx.

Just tell them Caroline Peacher sent you."

What? Caroline Peacher? That is the name I saw written out in my spirit.

Proverbs 3:5-6

Trust in the Lord with all your heart and lean not on your own understanding; in all you ways acknowledge Him, And He shall direct your path.

Key take away #42   He will not let you down, if you truly give in to Him and give it ALL to Him. Trust and obedience are big keys.

Chapter 43 **More of the book**

The Big Miracle   Part Two

Oh my, now I had to keep going because I knew I was on to something. I called the number and told them there was an open bed even though they were telling me it was sold out. I asked if I could give them a check when I got there and they said I could. Well ,they put down my name and I hung up knowing this was going in the right direction and by them taking a check it gave me a couple of days to see about the money.

I asked Gary if (worse case scenario) I could borrow $1000 from our joint business account for a couple weeks to do something I felt God was leading me to do.

"Sure" he said, "What for? May I ask?"

"To go to a writers conference day after tomorrow in North Carolina," I said

He looked at me puzzled and repeated what I had just told him. "A writers conference in North Carolina?" He asked.

"Yes" I said.

"I didn't even know you were a writer" he said

"Oh yes" I said grinning **"since Friday!"**

I went back to work and when finished pondered how I could possibly find $1,000 in 1 more day to pay for the conference so as not to actually borrow it let alone an additional amount for the flight on a $300 budget.

That was 5 o:clock and by then I was home I sat in my living room pondering the **Caroline Peacher** ,wrong number, blessing. I had not sat there 10 minutes when the phone rang.

"Hello" I said

"Hi, Sheri?"

"Yes"I said

"It's Dorita." said the caller in her thick southern accent

"I was just lying here, thinking about the car we bought from you and was feeling bad all of a sudden that we had not paid you. I was trying to take a nap, but it felt like I was wrestling with the Lord" she said.

She continued "It feels like we may have taken advantage of you. I know it has been a long time since we paid you anything on the Cadillac. We are going to give you money this week, in fact, tonight. Would $1,000 help you? I would like to send Steve (her husband) up later tonight and give you $1,000."

"Oh my, that is crazy, I mean, yes that is great! Thank you so much." I said.

I did not see that coming!

Romans 8:28

And we know that in all things God works for the good of those who love him, who have been called according to His purpose.

Key take away #43   He is amazing in His ways

Chapter 42   The Airplane Seat 15B

The Big Miracle part 3

Enthused about that miracle, the next day I called airline discount companies one after another. They were all over $500. I still only had $300 cash to work with for transportation. I finally found one through AirCanada that was $320 and I decided to go for it. It took me about 45minutes to go through the procedure and just as I punched in confirmation …

the screen went blank.

"Are you kidding me?"

I went through all the information one more time and when I finally reached the Air Canada flight to purchase I found out it was **sold out**.

Well, that confounded me and I changed to Expedia and tried another time. Well, every time I had tried that day it had been over $500 because of purchasing last minute. This time up came a flight from Des Moines through O'Hare airport in Chicago onto Charlotte for, drum roll please, **$300**.

There were three seats available and it showed me a picture of the fuselage seating and allowed me to choose the seat I wanted from what was left.

I had never had this option before so I chose the first one down the aisle available. It came back not available, so I tried the next seat of the three and it also came back unavailable.

Finally I tried the last one. I was discouraged and not sure there was going to be any seat available.

This seat was **15b.** I clicked it and it was accepted!

"Praise God!"

I was going the next day.

To get a flight I had to accept a flight one day early. I added a rental car option for a discount price but worried whether I would be allowed a car rental as I had an Iowa temporary paper license. This seemed like a good topic for prayer again as without a rental car I would not be able to make the two hour drive through the mountains to get to the retreat at Moravian Falls. I love to drive but needed a miracle for the rental company to actually allow me to secure a car with that type of paper license. I called them at the airport car rental company and they confirmed that a car could be rented BUT they did not accept paper licenses, only plastic. I reserved it under my license number but ...

well...

I put it in God's hand's.

He got everything arranged this far. What was turning a little piece of paper into plastic for the Lord?

Hebrews 13:6 So we say with confidence, "The Lord is my helper; I will not be afraid.

Key take away # 44   The Lord is willing to help if we just give it to Him and let Him grow our faith.

Chapter 45 **The Flight**

The Big Miracle   Part Four

I checked in and sat waiting for my flight . I love to watch people in an airport. They are so diverse and interesting to watch. As I was sitting there I noticed that the average traveler for that flight looked pretty worn , like they had traveled a long distance to get to that point. As I was making that assumption an exception to my assumption walked across the terminal and had a seat near the check in desk.

She really stood out from the rest of the travelers. She was fresh and perfectly appointed in a crisp white shirt, brown silk pants with fringe of beads at the bottom of their cropped leg. Her sandals had an interesting bead accent that complimented the pants she wore. Her hair was smartly styled with a very regal grayish white color. All in all she looked like I said , perfectly put together, enough for it to catch your eye and decide she looked like a professional. My attention soon went to others and shortly there after my flight number was called.

I checked my bag and made my way down the aisle to my seat which was 15b, the only seat allowed when choosing at the time of booking.

When I got to row 15 I was surprised to see the lady I earlier described was in the other seat in that row.

I asked if the empty seat was 15b and the lady said, "Please sit down, I have already seen in my spirit that you are supposed to sit here".

Well, that caught my attention and I sat down.

At that moment I thought my blessing/miracles had already happened.

Little did I know they were just beginning.

Psalm 44:21
Would not God search this out? For He knows the secrets of the heart.

Key take away #45   God can arrange the seemingly impossible!

Chapter 46 **The Trip**

The Big Miracle   Part Five

We exchanged the usual Hi, how are you and names. Then we asked the other where they were going. She said she was flying in to Charlotte a day early for a writers conference.

I said, "That is really something as so was I."

"Really?" she said, "Mine is actually two hours away from there in Moravian Falls."

"Wow! So is mine." I said. "I came in a day early for the same conference."

"Really?" she exclaimed. "Why are you coming in early? I am coming in early because I do not want to drive. I am afraid to drive and figured I needed the extra time to make it work."

"Wow!" I said, "I came in early because I have a car rented, love to drive but do not know if they will actually let me do it in my name as I have a temporary paper license."

" You are the answer to my prayer," she said. "I prayed for a driver. And you are the answer to my prayer."

I said, "My prayer, I was praying , was for someone who could actually rent the car with a good plastic license!"

I couldn't believe it. We talked for the next 7 hours. I could not get enough of her spirit filled stories. We stopped at a restaurant and chatted till we thought we should get back on the road to get in to the lodge before dark.

We got along very well and I gave her a brief tour of Moravian Falls as I had been there before. We checked in and found a note that we were in the second lodge a night early for no extra charge. I guess God and Caroline Peacher had all the details covered. It meant we were rooming at the very same building.

Researching that miracle after the fact shows for that year, 20,000 persons a day fly into the Charlotte, NC Airport.

Many, many flights a day fly from O'Hare to Charlotte.

The average flight from Des Moines to Charlotte at that time was $480 Round Trip.

Extra night of lodging is not usually free.

Rental cars always require plastic credit cards.

Best friends for life usually take a bit of time to build.

Writers usually write for a period of time before going to a conference.

$1,000 conferences usually cost $1,000.

The odds of persons from two different states flying on the same flight from O'Hare to Charlotte sitting side by side that each flew in a day early because of a problem that each had the answer to the other persons prayer is astronomically inexplicable without God.

That built my faith so BIG . I now can pray and believe for anything.

Mathew 19:26

But Jesus looked at them and said With Men this is impossible but with God ALL things are possible.

Key take away ALL things are possible with Jesus!

Chapter 47 **The Books**

Joy filled ,we went to the most beautiful setting in the mountains and enjoyed, with the other 18 aspiring Christian authors, the testimonies of faith, that would later inspire and fill the pages of many Christian books yet to be written.

The books that God wanted written.

The books that He planned and orchestrated through our faith down to the smallest detail.

The books He arranged completely for those of us who stepped out in faith.

This is how my writing journey began. I hope you enjoyed this book that was made entirely possible through content and deed by our mighty and beautiful, and detail oriented, God Himself.

His love is ENORMOUS, His Spirit is TRUE!

How to connect with this ministry...

*I*nformation on how to reach Sheri to speak at your conference or church can be found below. She has a diverse background having been in education, television, construction. She has many interesting, inspiring, fun stories that glorify the Lord. Ordained in 2009, her prophetic gifting, seer and healing anointing is received well in large or small group settings. She loves to magnify the Lord and speaks of His supernatural healings, visions, dreams, miracles and events as experienced in her life.

Her books can be purchased at book stores nationwide or ordered on Amazon or the

Blessings Soup Kitchen Facebook group.

Proceeds from this book go to

STARR workforce inc/Blessings Soup Kitchen

228 East Main, Ottumwa, Iowa 52501 (next page)

Phone: (641) 777-7997

Email: prayitforward7777@gmail.com

Support for the following ministries can be mailed to STARR workforce inc address above; All profits of this book to;

501 3c non profit groups to include the following;

STARR industries (homeless rehabilitative industries)

Blessings Soup Kitchens

Sheri Locke Smith ministries

Mom Shirley's Bread Recipe from God

5 pounds white flour

5 quarts warm water

5 handfuls of sugar

5 pinches of salt

5 hand scoops of margarine

5 packets dry active yeast

Take the warm water and place in bowl. Place yeast in warm water till it becomes active then place the butter, salt and sugar in until dissolved. Slowly add the flour until thoroughly mixed in. When dough has doubled, punch down with greased hands and turn over in bowl until doubles in size again. After it raises Turn dough out onto floured surface and gently knead to remove any air pockets. Divide into five equal loaves, place into greased pans. Bake at 400 for 20 minutes or until bread crust is well done. Turn out onto racks to cool.

Slice and enjoy.

Let everything that has breath

praise the Lord!

Praise the Lord!

For His Glory!

Made in the USA
Monee, IL
22 January 2022